ANCHOR BOOKS

POETS FROM THE UK 1999

Edited by

Kelly Deacon

First published in Great Britain in 1999 by
ANCHOR BOOKS
Remus House,
Coltsfoot Drive,
Woodston,
Peterborough, PE2 9JX
Telephone (01733) 898101

HB ISBN 1 85930 669 1
SB ISBN 1 85930 664 0

FOREWORD

Anchor Books is a small press, established in 1992, with the aim of promoting readable poetry to as wide an audience as possible.

We hope to establish an outlet for writers of poetry who may have struggled to see their work in print.

The poems presented here have been selected from many entries. Editing proved to be a difficult task and as the Editor, the final selection was mine.

Anchor Books - Poets from the UK 1999 is a compilation of poetry which has been assembled using the work of poets who reside in the United Kingdom.

The poems vary in style and content, ranging from what they like about their town or city to pleasant memories in life and the joys of the world today.

Each poem is a unique inspiration reflecting on the true emotions from each poetic heart.

A delightful collection for one and all to read time and time again.

Kelly Deacon
Editor

CONTENTS

EXHILARATION

The first light of dawn on a glorious new morn,
alerts drowsy senses to the birth of a day.
Unsure of surroundings feeling deep rhythmic poundings,
of a heart pumping precious warm blood to the fray.

Slowly opening eyes view the welcoming sight,
of the angelic photographed face of my love.
Tender proof of smooth passage through turbulent night
safe arrival one more special gift from above.

Striding inspired through the tear-dropping dew,
tingling-fresh breeze persuades former pale cheeks to glow.
Whilst the early-bird choir in their usual pew,
sing a sweet serenade on the opening show.

The sun's golden beams instigate smiling faces,
transforming blank windows to rare sparkling jewels.
Brave souls now emerge sending pets through their paces,
and peace reigns at breakfast as night passion cools.

At poignant sound of hooting owl the brimming heart doth overflow.
Alone upon the misty heath I tiptoe tall to touch the moon.
Whilst whispering winds confer with trees of mysteries we will
                                        never know.
This tiny speck in nature's plan portrays a universe in tune.

Frank Smiley
Bedfordshire

BARTON SPRINGS

Enfolded in those towering hills
where springs like silver flow.
A place so quiet and peaceful
somewhere we often go.

Through meadows and their swaying grass
wild flower with fragrant beauty.
This unspoilt spot a haven still
to guard it is our duty.

So children and their children too
can still see hills of green.
Not spoilt by ravages of time
and scars where man has been

Back now through woods and leafy glades
down paths we know so well.
The welcome coolness of its shade
it's time to pause and dwell.

On childhood memories that we hold
so dear in many ways.
Of times we spent with friends we knew
those thoughts of happy days.

Alan J Vincent
Bedfordshire

PERCY WOOD PIGEON

It is quite amazing and absurd
how much love I could have for a bird.
Brought to me when one week old
in the palm of my hand I could hold
this orphan chick, with regard feeding
I could tell he had good Woodstock breeding!
Growing daily and with feathers sleek.
The time had come for him to fly
with shed door open, so he'd try
to join the others flying free
it was time to take his leave from me.
Two days away, I was so sad
just wondering what fate he had.
Next morning tears of joy were shed
Percy flew in on my head!
Scanning the sky, in sun and rain
I stood with him to hold the grain.
Sat on my arm, like a trusting child
he was truly happy in the wild.
Then nature took its cruel course
and took away his fine life force.
A hawk had pinned him to the ground.
Too late to save my precious friend
our time together was at an end.
I buried him under the Christmas tree
it was time to take his leave from me.
It is quite amazing and absurd
how much love I could have for a bird . . .

Carolyne Calder
Berkshire

BEYOND THE STREAM

We looked towards the village
as we stepped down from the bus.
Beyond the stream and hump-backed bridge
the place that was once home to us.

After forty years of absence
at a distance it looked the same.
So contented, so peaceful
as we walked along the dusty lane.

It was forty years ago, we said
that me and my pal Titch
would leave this tiny village
and return when we were rich.

We would go out into the world
for our cache of gold to find
to make our mark. And let
our reel of fate unwind.

We toiled and tried
our coil of fate unwound.
But only hardship we endured
no cache of gold was found.

So towards the village
our old friends there to find.
Brother can you spare a cup of tea
would you be so kind.

But we found only strangers
no one that we knew.
Where are our pals, we asked
they have all gone too.

From this tiny village
with a stream and hump-backed bridge.

K Coleman
Buckinghamshire

THE DANCE OF LIFE

Life is a dance from beginning to end
A *Tango, Jive, Foxtrot* and *Twist*
For time will *March* on
As we *Sway* through the years
We *Beguine* as we first exist.
Beat of our hearts, *Rythm* of life
A *Roundelay* of *Ragtime* acoustics.
The *Cha Cha* of childhood
A *Fling* then the *Blues* -
Calypso and *Swing* - times of bliss.
Gospel inspiring, *Lancers* of old
Can Can on the *Rock* everyday
The *Reel* and the *Caller*
Of *Country* in tune
The *Bop, Hop and Rap Break* away;
The *Soul* ever seeking
The *Ballad* that speaks
A *Ballet* to *Glide* life's pathway
The *Quickstep* of being
All *Square* now, complete
A last *Waltz* at the end of our day.

Joan Heybourn
Buckinghamshire

THIS LAND

I love this land from whence I came
But strangely enough, I feel betrayed
Not because of the vibrant green of the hills
Or the depth of valleys, the ocean so still
Nor as I look up, the blackness of sky at night
At the beautiful moon, that helps give us light
The mighty sun, shedding her heat
These things I love - in my heart will keep
In awe of all this, a solitary tear on my face
So how, with breathtaking visions, did we fall from grace?
I am ashamed as we stand with weapons of war
Such loss of life - I cry 'What for?'
As the ocean fills with crimson blood
The deep green valleys awash by a mighty flood
Circling every seed that was ever sown
Leaving the land barren, nothing more can grow!
Before it's too late, can I ask of you
Why can't we live - and let others live too?

Christine Peers
Cambridgeshire

SPARE A THOUGHT

Spare a thought for children in war-torn far off places
Sheltering from conflict horror with saddened little faces,
Spare a thought for nursing staff dealing with the sick each day
Helping with the patient care and soothing ills away,
Spare a thought for the blind man when he taps along the street
Avoiding unseen objects that he's inclined to meet.
Spare a thought for the elderly living on meagre pensions
Accepting old age with dignity and hopeless expectations.
Spare a though for babies that Mothers cannot feed
Suffering malnutrition both in desperate need,
Spare a thought for everyone that lives upon this earth
Give generous love and charity, no matter what it's worth.

Dusty Sutherland
Cambridgeshire

A SECRET PLACE

Where is this secret place of mine
The charm of which cannot decline?
It's been a constant joy to see
How it remains unceasingly.

The fun I had there as a child
Those teenage years when running wild,
I cycled down the lanes so free
Had picnics down beside the sea.

Down lovers lanes where hand in hand
Our future happy life we planned.
I watched my children growing fast,
How quickly all the time has passed.

Our hopes and dreams are also here
But sometimes plans are never clear.
We cannot know what lies ahead
But by the Lord we shall be led.

Still no-one can my space invade
To spoil my treasured masquerade,
It holds the memories old and new
Not visible for all to view.

But everyone both rich and poor
Can from this place great pleasure draw.
It is not difficult to find,
You have the key to unlock your mind.

Angela Hudson-Peacock
Cambridgeshire

DON'T

Don't treat me like a fool, because my legs don't work.
Don't treat me like an oaf because I'm deaf.
Don't think I have no mind, because my eyes are blind.
Don't shun me for being different and looking like I do.
It's not my fault I look like me, or yours you look like you.

Don't mock me when I shuffle, when I stagger, when I walk.
Don't giggle when I stammer, when I stutter, when I talk.
Don't hurt me, if I can't look the way you want me to.
Don't blame me for being me and I won't blame you for being you.

I may not talk, I may not walk, I might not hear you speak.
But I am me and I can think. Just ask *me*, what do *you* think?
Speak to me, to me as me. Not to them, to them as him.

Geoff Donovan
Cambridgeshire

THE IMPORTANT YEARS

Oh, where have they gone, those childhood days?

Of horse and cart and leisurely ways.
The times we had, when we were young
the tunes we whistled and the songs we sung.

Summer days spent by the riverbank.
In tents that leaked and boats that sank.
Diving in and climbing out
that's what life was all about.
We only lived for the sunny days and
never thought to mend our ways
as we lay about in the summer haze.

When autumn came so rich and brown.
Excuses we made for not going to town.
Saturdays were kept for going out
looking for conkers, 'Here's one!' we'd shout.
Diving through pockets to find some twine
Jack Benson shouts 'Here! Try mine!'
The knot at the end was tied with speed
'Who'll make the hole in the conker?' came the cry in need.

'I've got a nail but it's a little bit bent,'
said John, making sure they knew it was lent.
'Quick, find a gatepost. Now hold it tight,
and slam down the rock with all your might.'
A hefty swipe and the nails gone through
'Blooming heck! My jacket too!
My mum will kill me that's for sure.
Never mind, come on lads, let's get some more.'

Thomas Roy McLeod
Cheshire

FASHION IN THE PARK

Onto the track saunter
Co-ordinated couples, swaying casually in green goretex.
Rainbow children zigzag, cagoules colour-clashing,
While senior comrades bob in woolly hats.
Beware the stick stabbers, calves gaiter-gripped,
As they mark their route, warning off novices.
The binocular brigade pause and pose;
Green wellies plod on.
Ahead, fell boots flex, laces flicking;
Shoulders nonchalantly shrug, and shift
Packs, preening their array of zips, pockets and flaps.
The show strides on, with gloves gesticulating
- a sign, a stile, a view!

Liz Owen
Cheshire

SUNSHINE

We woke up one morning
all shivery and cold.
Pulled on a woolly
and really felt old.
Why can't winter be kinder?
With just a small ray of sun?
To warm up our old bones
then we won't feel so glum.
But the weather's surprising
for lo and behold
the winter has fled
and so had the cold.
The bright sun is shining,
there's flowers in bloom.
Gone are the shivers
gone is the gloom.
We bask in the sunshine
humming all day.
And hope in our hearts
it is here to stay.
Crisp washing on lines,
blowing in a warm breeze.
Sweet childish laughter
and birds in the trees.
If only our lives
could be like the sun.
shining and warming
and a whole lot of fun.

Cozzetta Smith
Cleveland

LETTER TO A SOLDIER

While you are far away dear, I think of you each night
and wonder why it had to be, why you were made to fight.
The war it seems will last an age and prevents you being near
when all I really want is to have you standing here.
Your children sure do miss you, but think their daddy brave.
However, sometimes when I look at them with faces sad and grave
my heart it aches to have you home, to see you hold them near.
A little girl that cries for you, a little boy so dear.

I pray to God 'Please take care of one we love so much'
and if a bullet hits you, pray your heart, it does not touch.
For war and fighting do mean death but it's an awful shame
that men have got to lose their lives if the enemy can aim.
For the man that fires the bullet might be really nice like you
with a wife that's waiting home for him, and maybe children too.
He could have medals on his chest to say he too is brave
and just like you while he fights on, a life or two he'll save.
It could just be that this same man who's fighting to survive
is hoping just the same as you, to get back home alive.
But to you he is the enemy whom you'll meet and maybe kill
then leave there where he falls, a body on a hill.

Oh! How I wish this war would cease and man would learn to
live in peace.

M Pearson-Davies
Cleveland

REFLECTIONS

As I view the past in retrospect,
there's not much I'd alter I suspect.
A small thing here, and another there,
but basically I'd do the same I declare.
There's certainly places I wish I'd seen,
to countries abroad I wish I'd been.
Now I do not like to travel far,
my health is so often below par.
Regrets I confess I have a few,
as over the year's long past I review.
The longer I live it seems to me
nothing is as important as it used to be.
All the longings I had when younger,
are memories of things I need no longer.
My thoughts are now of the life to come,
when I have to account for the things I've done.
The people I loved who passed on in pain,
I wonder, will I see them again?
My faith grows stronger the longer I live,
I hope I don't fail when able to give.
I'm pleased I don't know the date of my death.
I'll have faith in my Saviour till I draw my
last breath.

Lilian Naisbitt
Co Durham

SWIFTS

You glorious aerial sprites that rend the sky
with slender pointed wings and piercing cry.
Exultantly, indomitably free . . .
Each year you come from far across the sea
and bring me with your presence pure delight.
As tirelessly you ply from morn till night
your never-ending task of seeking food.
To still the clamour of your ravenous brood,
fulfilling your life's purpose ere you leave
once more for warmer climes. Then I must grieve;
The air that rang with your excited screams
so strangely silent and deserted seems . . .
Brief apparitions from another sphere.
Of all birds you are to my heart most dear.

Evelyn Scott Brown
Cornwall

THE MESSENGER OF SPRING

Every year I really listen hard
out in the country and in my back yard.
Under budding trees the bluebells bloom
and blushing spring brides smile up at their grooms.
New-born lambs caper and gambol,
tiny thorns grow along the new brambles.
A warm breeze whispers and caresses the flowers
which in turn are kissed by light showers.
Hold on! What's that I heard?
Was it the call of that elusive bird?
No! It seems I'm out of luck once more,
so I'll go on a trip (which I adore)
across to France to relax and rest
(these are the things that I do the best).
And while my vitality starts to renew
I finally hear that darned cuckoo!

Margaret Phillips
Cornwall

CHILDHOOD MEMORIES

Just above the fireplace the flickering gaslight burns
In every corner of the room dark shadows cause concern.
Oil-lamp on the table, its light not bright enough
Outside the net-lace windows the day has turned to dusk.

In the range the fire glows, above the kettle stands
Atop the mantle a wooden clock and a china one-man band
Brass candlesticks all clean and bright, candles long since gone
By the letters neatly stacked a small brass dinner gong.

The smell of good wax polish, a whiff of paraffin
Condensation all around as the kettle starts to steam
There's a bright red step outside the door, rubbed until it gleams
Which indicates to passers-by, inside the house is clean.

Wireless on the sideboard with the Home and Light broadcast
At the back the batteries, made with see-through glass
Dick Barton and his agents,.Bill Cotton and his band
We sat there, all mesmerised, by all those magic sounds.

In the kitchen on the wall, an old tin bath would hang
A mangle near the pantry was always close at hand
The copper in the corner was where the washboard could be found
And irons for the pressing of, on a pyramid would stand.

There was one room within the house that no one dares abuse
And that was the parlour room, for it was rarely used
On high days and holidays a fire would be lit
Jjust to rid the damp and smell, and warm it up a bit.

These are just some memories that my childhood brings to mind
Hard working people who were rough but often kind
Some say, they were the good old days, but this I can't agree
Today with this technology, life is just a breeze.

Keith Onslow
Cornwall

COMMUNION

Lucifer contrived to meet an angel
on a dark and deserted city street.
He tempted her, just as he tempted Jesus,
arraying earthly treasures at her feet.

Her ears were deaf to his entreaty;
there was no trace of fear in her eyes,
and blessed with a smile that conjured paradise,
love's needle pricked the Lord of the Flies.

Gazing like a priest upon a miracle,
he felt the ghost of his former grace.
Reaching out a hand that ached to crush her
he traced a silver talon 'cross her face.

As she raised her gentle hand to enclose his
he trembled with the pain of perfect love.
For an endless, fleeting moment he remembered
all that was lost when he betrayed the dove.

She watched his eyes flicker in the shadow
with the cold, unholy light of tragedy.
On her knees she prayed to Michael the Archangel
for the mercy and the strength to set him free.

'Repent your evil ways,' the angel pleaded,
'seek forgiveness from the Lord, your God.'
But with those words she sensed that she had lost him;
for too long now his hand had held the rod.

He could not renounce the power that he wielded
though his kingdom fed on treachery and lies.
With a curse that cracked the air like thunder
the prince of darkness quickly faded from her eyes.

Michael Rollins
Cumbria

YUGOSLAVIA, EVEN ANGELS CRY

The sky above, sheds tears of sorrow-
whilst angels, bow their heads in shame.
'Neath grey sky, people are sadly dying -
man, has caused such terrible pain!

There is no sound, of human laughter -
or birds singing, in the sky.
The only sound, is that of grieving
'As ordinary people, lay down to die!'

Hear the sound, of human torment,
hear their anguish, throughout the night.
Tired limbs and war-torn bodies -
everywhere, such a sad, sad sight!

The sky above, sheds tears of sorrow -
Darkness, hides the grief and pain.
'What, will happen on the 'morrow?'
'Will God's light, ever shine again?'

Grey clouds scurry, across a weary sky -
as children, feel the pain of war.
The Heavens, heave an awesome sigh.
'Will Angels cry, forever more?'

The sky above, sheds tears of sorrow -
Man, should hang his head in shame.
'Why, are these things meant to happen?'
'There's no-one, wants to share the blame!'

There is no echo, of human laughter.
A mist of death, palls nearby.
The only sound, is one of sorrow
'As ordinary people, lay down to die!'

And as I sit here in my freedom
I join the Angels, as they cry . . .

Thomas Ian Graham
Cumbria

CHAPEL HILL

My mum wrote about this wondrous place
where there's nothing but peace and quiet to face.
This is where my loved ones' ashes are lain
deep in the ground and free from all pain.

I took a walk down there only last week
to see if I could find the peace that I seek.
As I stood there looking down, a magpie flew by
I recited the rhyme 'One for sorrow, two for joy' and I just had to cry.
Not just for myself, but for all the others
who have lost their fathers, mothers and brothers.

Life now is so pressured and run at full pelt.
But everything seemed to stop while on the grass I knelt.
There was no sound of cars speeding by,
just the sound of the birds sat in the trees so high.

As I took in the quiet and stillness around me, I felt a sense of peace
and said a prayer for all the world's hostilities to cease.
If only people could find the time to spare
to come and reflect here, much better they would fare.
Because they too would feel so much calm
and although alone, they would come to no harm.
For Jesus would care for them in this special Garden,
and all their sins and faults he would surely pardon.

Judy Buxton
Cumbria

THE CLERK OF HEAVEN

Upon his stool the Clerk of Heaven sits.
He scribbles in his ledger each man's deed.
He gathers all the evidence from life
against a day the Master has decreed.
Beside the stool a *chest of laughter* rests
containing all life's merriment and mirth,
the record of how well men understood
the day which holds no smile is lost on earth.
About him roses crowd which never fade.
Amid their velvet petals tears are kept;
the evidence of when we cried for joy
or when, through sorrow, bitterly we wept.

One page of Heaven's diary turns each day
revealing our appointment with the Clerk.
(Though many pass through death's grim door with ease,
still men fear death, like children fear the dark.)
We take our place on Heaven's golden scales
by whose wide beam are balanced judgements made.
Against the *good* surrounding every man
his *infamy* is counterpoised and weighed.
Perhaps the failing pendulum mid-way
between *acceptance* and *rejection* lies.
Then how we search for one kind thought, a laugh
or tear to tip the scale towards Paradise!

Our life is now; tomorrow is unknown;
The tally of our yesterdays complete.
To fling the gates of Heaven wide, each man
may need the merit gained *this* day, for weight.

John M Beazley
Cumbria

TIME

Do we really see
the time that passes.
Or just sit here
with tinted glasses.
Leave everything for another day.
'Do it now' - 'Me! No way!'
'We'll do it tomorrow
there's plenty of time.'
'What's wrong with today?'
'No! tomorrow's fine.'

When we are young
we've the time it seems
enough to fulfil
our hopes and dreams.
But as the years fly quickly past
and each one could be the very last.
Maybe the things
that weren't urgent then
have changed the word
from *if to when.*

K M Riley
Derbyshire

THE DERBYSHIRE DONKEY STONE

Rows of washing on the line.
Lines of boiled white cotton.
Soapy suds from dolly-tubs
Wash lines with wooden props on.

Hot water from the dolly-tub
Splashed out across the yard.
Stiff bristled brushes scrubbing flags.
Oh heck, the work was hard!

The carpet hung over the wall.
The dust well beaten out.
The carpet-beater swinging
Would give it such a clout.

Then for the final touches
On the edge of step and sill.
A creamy line of Donkey Stone
Made the yard look brighter still!

Shirley Williamson
Derbyshire

STAUNTON HAROLD

Staunton Hall stands majestically high,
looking aloof, down on the scene below.
Like a stately cedar, erect and tall
always aware of an approaching foe.

The court crowned with a medicean lion,
rich red brick walls and ornamented stone.
Two gate piers surmounted with hound and stag
a medieval house I'd like to own.

Staunton Church, just a few yards away.
A splendid example in the Gothic style.
With magnificent woodwork and paintings,
such a pleasure to view from the aisle.

The two curving lakes, below the lawns
surrounded by shrubs and trees most rare.
Fishermen with their rods awaiting
to catch some fish, but disturb if you dare.

The Shirley family, steeped in history -
involved with politics, treason and crime.
Improving the hall and building a church
battling on through troubled times.

Joyce Wakefield
Derbyshire

FOR MUM

I love you more than words can say
I love you more each passing day.
We've supported each other for many years
and I'll be there to talk you through your fears.
I'll be there for you night and day
when you need me
you just need to say.
Whatever happens I'll be there for you
I'll support you in whatever you do.
I just want to say how much I care
and if you want a shoulder to cry on
I will always be there.
Just remember how much I love you
and I'll be there always for you.

Linda Casey
Devon

THE UNTOUCHABLES

Hungry, muddled, the dazed refugees.
All fugitives flee.

Crying, dirty, the homeless are scared.
All displaced travel.

Cold, sore, aching and empty.
The outcasts search.

The old, young, able and disabled,
Settle as exiles.

In war, peace, with little or no hope.
The refugees survive.

Debra Neale
Devon

THE PINK BALLOON

A balloon careering down the street
pink in colour, to me, did meet.
I followed in high winds as it went
uncontrolled on where it was sent.

It was in sudden surges and currents caught,
by invisible fingers it was sought.
Which flung it high, then climbing walls,
as if jet-propelled it falls.

With a life of its own, under wheels of cars,
next reaching for the stars.
Into the churchyard it did travel
I, watching as it bumped over the gravel.

In its final throes it went pop,
as on a rose thorn it met its lot.
I thought how much this compares with life,
when dreams come to strife.
They rise and fall in ebb and flow
and dash the seeds that we did sow.

Douglas Dart
Devon

GUITAR LOVER

My lover he strums an old guitar
and sings the blues late at night
While a saxophone plays to itself,
crooning of love and moonlight.

I know it'll be a long, long time
until he looks over at me
For I don't exist for him right now,
the guitar, his lover will be.

He sings old lonely cowboy songs
of love long lost - all gone away
And the air over Virginia;
he hopes to visit there one day.

His guitar seems to cry for him,
tears running down and away.
But when he stops the voice is stilled;
it's his voice in a way.

So I sit, cigarette in hand;
glass of beer in front of me,
Hardly tasted, listening hard
as my lover sings bluesy.

The saxophone is softer now -
the club will soon be shut,
But still the guitar cries to itself
until in its case it is put.

Then my lover returns to me,
in his arms holds me tight
For now my lover is all mine,
we'll make love by moonlight.

J Alban-Johnson
Devon

THE BLUEBELL WOOD

A carpet of blue to feast my eyes
so brilliant in colour, it almost defies
it can be real.
As I wend my way through the trees to a clearing
the early morn's mist is fast disappearing.

The scene is uncanny, for the ground is as blue
as the sky.
I search for a path to wend my way through
to this beautiful spot of azure blue.
There are but a few who know of this spot
deep in the wood, they have forgot.

A small piece of God's garden, here all alone,
where all these bluebells have profusely grown.
There are no rampant feet to trample them down
no busy fingers to pick and throw them around.

I choose my way carefully, so as not to tread
on any one petal of their lovely head.
Upon reaching the centre of the glade
I sit upon a boulder, that seems to have been laid.

Just for me alone, to sit and rest
to gaze upon a place that is surely blessed.
To feast my eyes on a carpet of blue
that I feel has been made especially for me,
and perhaps for you too.

Helen Phillips
Devon

LOVERS

The night is quiet
nobody around.
I lie here and think
I see you in bed.
All quiet and sleeping,
I see you clearly.
You look so innocent,
in your dreams.
You move slightly
the covers fall.
I reach my arm out,
and run it slowly down
your back.
Your skin so soft and hot.
You move again,
the covers fall.
I see your naked form.
I curl up next to you
you reach out for me.
We touch, we kiss,
we melt into each other.
These moments I love,
just like complete heaven.
You then awake,
I look into your eyes
I see love, I see trust.
I see future, I see us.

Anna French
Devon

KISMET

Now I'm in your hands. I
mere mortal can do no more.
I surrender this sense of self
which testifies we control our own destiny.
Control it thro' the matter mass called brain
                    I give it up.

Now I bow to you. Send
the design you have for me.
I relinquish my claim of rule
which signifies I'm master of circumstance.
Master of all the bafflement called life
                    I let it go.

Now I abrogate. I
let my spirit kneel to you.
Force it to accept your will
my drive be nullified for you to guide
my existence thro' a maze of management
                    I resign.

But even as I waive this
claim I rebel against it.
Revoke the aeons of world files
which pictures man as frail, powerless, lacking.
Who totals not one micro-second of infinity
                    And makes it thus.

Susan McGraw
Dorset

AUTUMN

When autumn casts its soulful spell
I love to stroll o'er dale and dell
drinking in a lustrous sea
of colours, glowing vibrantly
My senses reel in sheer delight
and revel in the wondrous sight
of yellows, reds and golden brown
in which my cares and sorrows drown
All seasons are uniquely clad
in colours gay and colours sad
but colours cast in perfect rhyme
make autumn's stay my favourite time.

Geoffrey Lindley
Dorset

EYES OF FEAR

He looked so alone, his eyes full of fear;
Surrounded by bracken, the wind in the trees,
The sound of barking dogs, people shouting,
Their voices high.
Far away, but yet so near,
They laughed, they cheered, I was in tears
The fox

He crouched low to the ground
Creeping slowly away from the noise,
His ears pinned back, his tail low down;
Trying desperately to make no sound.
Closer they came, men, women, boys,
I prayed for him
The fox

He stopped, he shivered, he looked so small,
Alone he stood, no one at his side,
His ears pricked up, he turned his head,
Waiting, wondering, watching.
The noise abated, he stood up tall;
Slowly he realised he had not died,
Was it my prayer?
The fox

Jean Tapping
Dorset

MAY

Lace-like blossom embroiders nesting hedgerows
As morning mist shrouds a sentinel rabbit
Nervously alert for any predatory attack.
Brooding oaks flesh out gaunt and splintered branches
Overhanging restless cows pestered by newly-swarming flies.
A cloistered stillness echoes in the shadowy copse
Bluebell carpeted and hauntingly scented
Waves of petals breathlessly stirring at the slightest breeze
A sanctuary for forlorn cuckoo call
Timeless in its repeated pleading
Interspersed with the machine-gun rattle of a pneumatic woodpecker.

Gleams of oriental colour tell-tale trace a wandering pheasant
Whilst candyfloss clouds casually saunter overhead.
Sunlight sparkles in quietly rippling streams
Where spring-cleaned gravel glistens in scrubbed cleanliness.
Swallows loop and chase across a spacious sapphire sky
A fork-tailed fly-past of compressed energy
Preoccupied with flowing patterns of aerobatic ease.
Slowly warming fields sway with new-found vigour
Overthrowing the coffined sloth of winter
The pace of living rushes towards the flowered pleasure of fruition.

Christopher Korta
Dorset

ELEMENTS

Sun and air, warm and cool,
Son and heir: lover fool,
Sun and air, hot and humid,
Son and heir: colourful vivid,
Sun and air, gold and blue,
Son and heir: I love you.

Air and sun, balmy heady,
Heir and son: bold and steady,
Air and sun, breezy glaring,
Heir and son: clever daring,
Air and sun, tempest grill,
Heir and son: love me still . . .

L P P
East Sussex

SOMEONE SPECIAL

She would toddle along with a pram full of dolls,
Everyone of them, neat as a pin.
'You mustn't get cold - it's a nasty old day,'
She would whisper, whilst tucking them in.
She was always the same - such a dear little soul.
I have known her since she as a tot,
When her brother was born, she would sit by his side,
And sing him to sleep in his cot.
They grew up together - 'twas lovely to see,
Then, one day I looked, and I saw there were three!
She never complained of the muddle they made,
And hurried to tidy it up,
She is just the same now, when she brings me my tea,
Taking care of my very best cup.
All the shopping gets done, and there's never a fuss,
When the queue is so long that she misses the bus.
She is just like a daughter is my little Sarah,
I can never repay what I owe to my carer.

Tiger
East Sussex

FIREHILLS

Undulating, so elating, where green doth meet the blue
Sea that's so relentless, it's not as I once knew.
Crashing, bashing, smashing this land we want to save,
Eaten by the ebb and flow and swallowed by the wave.

Undulating, so elating, to walk across the green
Where once the Coastguard Cottage for many years had been.
Now gone to sea and gone to dust, beyond the rocky cave.
Coast eroded, signs foreboded, eaten by the wave.

Undulating, so elating, this land that saw my birth,
To walk up there, full joy and mirth, upon that springy turf.
Now the lashing and the thrashing of the sea and all its skills
Have worn away, another day, of life on gold firehills.

Undulating, so elating, the Firehills where alight
Above the surf, next green of turf, in gold and crimson bright.
Awesome sight, nature's light, keeps up the hopeless fight,
Against the sea, that seems to be, that omnipotent might.

Nola McSweeney
East Sussex

FROM A SICK BED

As the breath of day passes
through the crippled lungs
of forgotten lives wasted,
idly scattered amongst the garbage.
Do we clutch frantically at life
as if snatching at the tide?

Or is it not too late:
to search,
to learn,
to realise
the playground of dreams
of childhood?

Turn away the workers' fear
and fly
upon the gossamer kiss
of an angel's breath.
To soar, to glide above the masses
on Blériot wings.
And to revel in the carnival
that lies within.

There is another place
beyond this hourglass,
beyond this skin.

Michael Wilson
East Sussex

ROAD RAGE

Sitting in the wine bar watching the world go by
As I sit I ponder and I wonder why
They rush around like mad men with never a moment to think
Never time to say 'Hello mate, would you like a drink?'

And then there is the motorist
Now, there's the strangest fellow!
He drives around at breakneck speed
And you'll hear him bellow
'What do you think you're doing,
You ignorant, stupid fool?'

If only he would calm down
And regain his cool!

Then he'd realise the truth
That speed can drive you mad
It really can distort the mind
Now, that is really sad!

He thinks he rules the highways
He thinks he knows it all
But one day he will realise
That he is 'the ignorant fool'!

S Friede
Essex

GLORY DAYS

Where are the wheels of yesteryear
That turned a merry tune?
Where are those heady summer days
That ended far too soon?

Where are the shining silver knights
The dragons that they slayed?
Where are the damsels in distress
The maidens that they saved?

Where are the bows and arrows
The horses and the guns?
Where is the false impression
Of how the west was won?

Where is the buried treasure map
That the pirates gave to me?
Where is the skull and crossbones
That ruled a bygone sea?

Where are the myths and legends
Enacted in my mind?
They're lost within a childhood
That's now so hard to find

Ian Falconer
Essex

WINNING

I spent the seven million
Without feeling any shame.
As winning it had given me
Five minutes worth of fame.

I held the all night parties
The food and wine they flowed.
I sent good causes presents
Bought by the wagon load.

I wore the sexy underwear
I bought designer clothes.
I had the liposuction done
Asked them to fix my nose.

I had my grey hair coloured
My bum tucked, underneath.
I had my double chin fixed
And purchased some new teeth.

I took to drinking cocktails
Every day, before eleven.
I thought I was the bee's knees
I thought I was in heaven.

I paid in cash for everything
It gave me such a thrill.
I'd spent the lot in no time
No need to make a will.

Ah! but were you really happy?
The moralists, they scream.
Yes, for I didn't have a penny
When I woke up from my dream.

Tricia Porter
Essex

To Be Free

My soul cries out to me
Release me from this life
Let me be free
Let me be the way I want to be

I dream of paradise
Maybe there I'll be free
I'll be able to speak
And people will listen

Don't look away
Hear what I have to say
I want to intrigue you
Make you forget yourself

I want to have the courage
To tell you how I feel
Not to conform
But to be free.

P Cerullo
Essex

GARETH

My desired is a chipmunk with spiky, yellow hair,
a goon's smile and a deranged stare.
He's the object of my affections; the apple of my eye.
The focus of attentions, my stomach's butterfly.

My darling Mr Bean,
of the deep, musical voice and sides so lean
jangles girlishly across the floor,
my friend's eye sore!

Now, with heart pounding and eyes like a saucer;
up I spring as my stomach flies over.
Sweaty and flushed I stutter a greeting,
gulp hard as my eyes are given a feasting.

Of this quirky child-man,
I dream and dream of sweaty nights and sex in a van.
My lunatic, lithe lover as I would have true,
bewitches me, entrances me, makes me shiver all through.

But in a second our brief exchange is over.
'Bye' I whine willing him to come closer.
Instead he exits with a beaming face,
dancing out the door to return to space.

Alice Smyth
Essex

THE BATTLE AT EDGE

Through darkened leaf-strewn lanes I strode
Where many horses once were rode.
Urgent, sweating, nostrils flaring,
Onwards before the break of day
And into yet more blood letting.

My footsteps crisp on cold, hard frost,
I hear the horsemen's cries; now lost;
And yet again, the clash of steel
I hear, as I go on my way.
And then the fallen.Cries so shrill.

I slip, I stumble in the dark
When haunting voices beg me hark
Unto their wailing, painful cries,
Of pikemen desperately at bay,
Losing the battle for their lives.

Upon the grave-like ground, supine,
My restless soul with their's entwine.
They rush towards me, masks of death,
I cannot have but time to pray,
Before they draw my last, short breath.

J G Ryder
Gloucestershire

THE LETTER

No fanfare of trumpets that day,
Just the postman on his rounds,
A letter, midst the junk mail,
My heart took leaps and bounds.
I recognised the writing,
It was hers without a doubt,
Trembling fingers opened slowly,
What I read, just knocked me out!
She wrote about her feelings,
How she treasured times with me
But sadly, 'the supreme sacrifice',
My dreams could never be.
I know she's someone special,
'The letter' tells me so,
Now I must go on living,
Though the pain I mustn't show.
Each time I read 'the letter',
Tears slowly fill my eyes,
My love for her, so strong will stay
Until this 'old man' dies!

T G Bloodworth
Gloucestershire

ALLURE

Can words dressed in mink and jewels flatter or persuade,
Or honeyed tongue or sensuous eye entice an innocent maid?
What act or word of fervid gaze
Can soothe the ear or look bedaze?

Does gaudy attire or provocative stance,
Incite a desire or wistful glance?
Can magnetic charm or pleasing guile,
Invite the reward of a coquettish smile?

Does a display of intelligence or show of wit,
Encourage the listener to submit;
Or does strutting the stage or prowess at sport,
Promote an interest and spirit transport?

Can an anxious manner play its part,
In capturing a gentle lady's heart?
Does shyness or modesty really enhance,
The allure of a feckless lover's chance?

Does the tone of voice or intent look
Impale the receiver on the hook?
Or can the blatant show of wealth
Entice the maiden off the shelf?

Whatever the sign that seems to attract;
(And before the allured enters a pact),
Pause to remember that outward show can
Mask the true feelings of the real inner man.

Be a wily trout, don't rise to the bait,
By accepting an offer on the first date.
Look deep into his eyes to fathom his role,
Because they reflect what's profound in his soul.

Bryan Colman Bird
Gloucestershire

CONSCIENCE

You stare, round eyed
from the corner of the room,
belly round, limbs like sticks,
your eyes saying
help me
help me.
There are no words
spoken
nor any needed
to describe your plight.
Whilst you stand there
mute
and pleading
the politicians talk
and dine
and toast each other's
brilliance
and we can switch you off.

Wendy Ray
Hampshire

NATURE'S GARDEN

I open my eyes, and gaze all around
I cannot believe there is hardly a sound
Just the buzz of the wasps, the flies and the bees
The rustle as wind passes through nearby trees.
The smell of the flowers, their colours so bright
They are turning their heads towards the sunlight
In my garden this is nature's wonder I see,
And I say to myself all this beauty is free.

Jeannie Smith
Hereford & Worcester

Mynydd Ddu - (Black Mountain)

Ancient stones, skeleton along the
backbone of the cat's back,
The patchwork globe rises and falls steeply below
across hills and waterfall.
In the distance the silver serpent gleams in the sun,
The ash branch shadows over a field,
grey fingers point towards the falcon's eye,
blackthorn punishes the skyward glow,
statued thorns bow, so undignified a-sight,
yet hold the beauty
and defy the bleakness
of every view.

Arfon Williams
Surrey

POEM TO A GENTLEMAN
(In memory of George Soloman)

Cast off from this mortal coil -
Gone now to a higher plain -
Above this world of flesh and bone.
Down the years of setting suns -
Like family and friends alike -
Touched by your humanity.
If I had a hat -
I would take it off to you.

K D Thomas
Hertfordshire

THE FLY

Patch looked up, and through one eye
Saw on his bone a huge big fly.
He crept towards the offending bug
Then took a pounce, landed on the rug,
Rolled on his back and again espied
That silver winged huge black fly.

Once again he crept along
The kitchen rug, his eye was fixed
Upon the bug, now on the chair.
He took a leap - the fly was not there.

Now this was getting Patch so mad.
Another leap - oops, sorry Dad!
Poor Dad was sitting on the floor.
'Now young Patch, enough - no more.'

Poor Patch, dejected, sat under the chair.
He will get that fly - but when or where.
Never mind, Patch, whatever you do
You are watching the fly
And God's watching you.

Don Friar
Hertfordshire

SUMMER LOVE

Soft on the pillow, white on white,
She lay her head that summer night,
Waiting for love to lift the latch
Slip quietly through the moonlit patch.
To slide beneath the silken sheet,
Where lips and bodies move to meet.
And as she lay and dreamed her dream,
Down through the woods and o'er the stream,
There came for her on silver steed,
Through trees and thickets with all speed,
A stranger, handsome, tall and fair,
With piercing gaze and flowing hair.
His velvet cloak of mossy green
Wrapped him around and so unseen
Quieter than the moonlight's rays,
Through darkest nights and brightest days,
He travelled fast his heart afire,
With love and longing and desire.
She never knew that e'er he came
To stroke her hair and call her name
His steed had slipped on mountain track,
The rider lay with broken back,
And there in moonlight, white on white,
He died for love that summer night.

Nell Arch
Hertfordshire

DEATH OF A TITAN

She died quickly
On this night of shame,
The glacial spear
Deep in her side.
Belief suspended they danced on,
The rich and famous
The infamous . . .
Drowning in champagne
Dying with laughter.
'She can't sink old chap.
It's unthinkable!'
But God is not mocked
Who cries 'Unsinkable' lies
And even a Titan dies.

Below the water line
The poor, blind in their poverty
Lost in the metal maze
Advance and retreat,
Meeting at every orifice
The suppurating icy sea.

Clawing the air
The wavering signals falter, fade . . .
In the throes of death
The Titan rolls
Lord, save our souls,
Lord, save our souls.

Toll now the knell
Sound the Lutine
In the silent deeps
A Titan sleeps.

Vera Morrill
Isle of Wight

HOMELESS

Do you feel the isolation,
Hopeless eyes awash with pain?
Staring into empty spaces -
Drowning in the frozen rain

Do you feel the desperation,
And the pride that won't be said?
Looking for a vacant doorway -
Ice cold pavement for a bed.

Do you feel the lonely sorrow,
Of a soul in black despair?
Looking deep into a cavern -
Finding nothing waiting there.

Can you hear the silent crying,
Hearts that bleed in barren space?
Can you touch the passing shadow -
Of a man without a face?

Do you feel a brief compassion,
As you throw a coin or two?
He - a man with no tomorrow -
You - a stranger passing through.

Mavis Joyce Green
Kent

THE PRISONER

Within the castle dark and bleak,
chained to the wall so cold and dank,
a single tear ran down the cheek
of the poor wretch as his head sank.

The fear of torture in his mind,
facing the terror, stretched on the rack,
and like so many of his kind,
the stripes from flogging on his back.

The cell door creaked, flung open wide,
in vain he shrank against the wall,
the guard with jangling keys by his side,
watched the man as he started to fall.

Dragged through passages musty and damp,
ever downward towards the sea,
until at last they crossed the ramp,
no chance now for the man to flee.

Seeing the ship, he knew his fate,
chained to an oar, he'd never be free,
time to confess was now too late,
for evermore a slave he'd be.

A Odger
Kent

THE MILKY WAY

At the end of a long and busy day
I leaned against the garden shed,
And gazed and gazed at the Milky Way,
Soon I found that my tiredness had fled.

When I thought of the size of those twinkling stars
And the millions of miles their light had travelled,
It was so amazing - could it really be true?
Did these heavenly jewels have planets too?

The longer I gazed, the more stars I saw,
I thought nature's beauty will never cease.
Was all this the product of cosmic law?
No! Only God creates beauty with peace.

K Sanderson
Kent

THE SHOOTING PARTY

Half risen was the wintry sun,
Yet gave no life to stark-etched trees,
Nor whispered warmth to frosted leas,
Nor smiled on men whose breath hung clouded,
Who trod the fields in gum boots green,
That crunched upon the hoar-frost keen.

Half risen was the pallid sun,
Yet touched not cold heart,
Nor stayed the hand on half-cocked gun,
Or warned of death upon the wing,
As feathered bundle fell, inert,
And crumpled upon the frozen earth.

Half risen was the watery sun,
Yet noticed not a life now gone,
Nor heeded bark of eager dog,
As into the distance men moved on.
Over furrowed fields, ground-mist shrouded,
Into the bleakness: Cold silence crowded.

V J Lawes
Kent

THE OTHER SIDE OF DARKNESS

From the other side of darkness
I watch you,
Silently sleeping,
Blissfully unaware
Of my nightly traumas.
You know nothing
Of the unseen terrors
That lurk somewhere
Deep within my soul.
You are oblivious
Of my longing
For the manifestations
Of daylight
To come, creeping
Through my window.

K Mather
Lancashire

A Year In The Garden

In winter, the garden lies bleak and bare,
No plants or flowers to tend with care.
The black, gnarled branches of the trees
Shiver silently in the breeze.
Lawns and hedges are drab and grey
On a dark and dismal wintry day.
Then soft, white snowflakes clothe the land
Creating winter wonderland.

In springtime, snowdrops dance in the breeze,
Crocus cluster beneath the trees.
Pansies with their happy faces,
Are springing up in many places.
And round lawn hedges, near and far
Grow primroses and primula.

All summer long the garden's ablaze,
A riot of colour beneath the sun's rays.
- Sweet smelling roses, bright coloured shrubs,
Fuschia in baskets, begonia in tubs,
Borders of peonies, lilies and phlox,
Salvia, pinks and sweet scented stocks,
Nearby, an arch of perfumed sweet peas
And purple clematis climbing the trees.

Summer has gone and flowers fade,
Autumn colours are on parade.
Leaves of orange and gold and brown,
Detached by the wind, come tumbling down.
They huddle together on the ground
Then twist and twirl as they blow around.
- But seasons come and seasons go,
When leaves have gone, it's winter once more.

M Alston
Lancashire

HOPE FOR THE NEXT MILLENNIUM

Oh you politicians, oh you men of war,
Why don't you remember what life is really for?
No mother's sons should have to lie
In filthy trenches where they die.
Men weren't born to kill each other,
Whatever their creed, or whatever their colour.
Life is for living, loving, for giving
Helping each other,
Not about bullets and killing,
For there aren't any winners in war,
So all you politicians, all you men of war,
In the next millennium
Make sure peace is all we know.

M Atkinson
Lancashire

THE FIJIAN SUNSET

The breeze gentle as a whisper
The ocean murmuring its timeless lullaby
Quickly and silently the night wrapped us in a velvet shawl
We stood in silence in wonder
And watched the glorious sunset
Reds, golds, greens, blues and oranges
We were a heartbeat away from heaven
Time stood still
Until this miracle slipped beyond the horizon

Freda Argyle
Lancashire

STREAMLINES

A time of roses assailed now
Frost has come,
Paleness and ice
Where once vine twisted
And vein surged
Air in its anguished swirling
Tricks all trying to look out again
Near that river
Where I might remember

This is a coast that cries
Where I climbed happy hills
As everything flowed
And flesh itself flowered
Following, I devoured the devout
Guessed the code of pressing wings
But cloud could not bear the unseasoned

I wondered whose wood
Witnessed the whispering
Whose stillness
Saw the shaft sing
Blossoms to break to love's alarm
And leaves going all away
In gold of laughter.

J Latham
Lancashire

ALMA'S SHOP

Still hoping for another fruitful day,
She flits the cobwebs from the sliding door,
Arranges handicrafts around the shop,
Assured the place looks picturesque once more.

While customers arrive, my special friend
Decides to utilise the waiting time
By knitting across a gamut of stitches which
She intertwines with saffron shade and lime.

A harvest of greenery dance the fandango near
Her window, keeping time with the dextrous tap
Of her needles, while the balls of wool are both
Cavorting causing chaos on her lap.

I watched the cheeky sun-shafts ruminate
Among the glossy hoops of her champagne hair,
She looked a picture without a diamond -
Picasso would have plumped for one so fair.

My lady is an art craft connoisseur,
Embroidery, fine lace, old china, these
Are woven in the fabric of her life,
To glimpse them, she would sail the seven seas.

Should you peruse around my Alma's shop,
You'll surely feel a liberal atmosphere,
No bribery, no pushing, no glum looks,
Only a pleasant smile and 'Thank you dear'.

S Hunter
Lancashire

A Refugee's Prayer

All I want is a bed
To rest my weary head,
A place to rest my feet.
Give me shelter from the heat.

Many miles I have come
From the home I loved so much.
Punched and kicked along the way,
Dreading every new day.

Will someone hear my silent prayer
And rescue me from this nightmare?
My baby may be born tonight.
All I want is a bed.

Eileen Norris
Lancashire

WRITTEN IN PORTUG-EASE

I'm a lazy four day beard
Retired bronzer
Lounging, peeling labels
From a half empty bottle of beer
Mirrored in the corner
By a humid, humming fridge
Busy encasing coldness
Around a one short six pack
Insulated in an ice box apartment
From a Mediterranean melee outside
A childish tidal cacophony
Past a fridge thick patio door
Twelve stories down
Boiling in a defrosted pool
And I smile in a heady condensation.

Matthew James Hardman
Lancashire

LOVE STORMS

When broken-hearted clouds appear,
heavy, in the arms of a storm,
they cry to wash away the fear,
my love is sheltered safe and warm.

Heavy, in the arms of a storm,
horizons lost by misty view,
my love is sheltered safe and warm,
the future path unclear, anew.

Horizons lost by misty view,
I'm speechless though bursting with song,
the future path unclear, anew,
such love as this cannot be wrong.

I'm speechless though bursting with song,
anything lesser would be naive,
such love as this cannot be wrong,
given time you too, can believe.

Anything lesser would be naive,
they cry to wash away the fear,
given time you too, can believe,
when broken-hearted clouds appear.

K G Watson
Lancashire

EASTER IN THE VILLAGE

Quiet churches fill with families,
Sunday school plays get underway.
Children dressed as donkeys with wobbly knees,
What an enjoyable day.

Outside the church,
Shops sell eggs for twice the price.
Mum opens her purse,
And 'I want three, yes that'll do nice.'

In the fields are new flecks of yellow and pink,
'The daffodils will be out soon' says Grandma.
Taking them some water from the sink.
She off loads some more pansies from the car.

Teenagers enjoy the sales in the shops,
Buying anything with a 'reduced' tag.
Shopkeepers in Thorton's work none stop,
Dishing out freebies, and putting eggs in special bags.

Katy Lomax (13)
Lancashire

THE ACTRESS

She's a tired old clapped out lady,
now sadly pushing ninety,
they say that she was once a star,
of the golden era of films and TV,
alas, no more parts come along her way,
time has since eclipsed her,
no longer the famous name of yesteryear,
the celluloid screen,
silently she's faded, long since into
obscurity,
it lingers on in memory,
photographs of her past is the only
thing she has to treasure,
of her life so long ago,
as a Hollywood actress.

Erika Carpenter
Lancashire

THE CHEEKY MONKEYS

The cheeky monkeys came today,
to make their mischief and have their way.
They cheekied their way through the door,
and unloaded some of their cheeky store.
They ran with ease up and down the walls,
saying: 'Look, no hands, I never fall!'
They poked their faces into my face,
and invaded my little, personal space,
then ran away gleeping with glee
at the shock they knew they'd given to me;
but who can be angry at their cheeky charm,
when the cheeky monkeys never mean any harm.
One minute they'll show you their bright blue bums,
the next they're be doing arithmetic sums
by counting their fingers and then their toes
one by one against their noses.
The cheeky monkeys had to go away,
when they'd done with all their fun play;
but if they should come and visit your home,
then do make their welcome pleasant and warm.
Let the cheeky monkeys in through your door,
and life won't be quite so dull any more.
They'll stop you from being so stuffy and twee
for the price of a banana and a cup of tea.

M B Smith
Leicestershire

COLOURS

The colours of the rainbow
Are beautiful to see,
They really are quite marvellous
And quite a mystery.
It has to do with water,
And it has to do with light,
Why worry how it comes to be
It's such a pretty sight.
We see these things around us
But do we take them in,
Or just take them for granted
Now that would be a sin.
We must learn to appreciate
What goes on all around,
From high up in the heavens
To low down on the ground.
All of nature's wonders
Are there for us to see,
We should make the most of them
They're absolutely free.

Ruth Smith
Leicestershire

NIGHTFALL

Snow driven, ivory lily pad;
swan on silver throne.
A silver frosted lake.

White hot candles fade.
The blackbird sings no more
in toffee burnt-almond glade.

Sunflower apricot sunset's gone;
no marmalade sky
or coppery beech nearby.

No reflection on rippling stream
just leaden skies.
Twilight; owl-light greyness.

Night falls; silhouettes dance.
A starless sky sleeps.
Heaven's blind gives rest a chance!

Annette Borrill
Lincolnshire

LOVE IN THE MOONLIGHT

When the moon is out at night
Romance is in the air
People stroll hand in hand
They never have a care
For there's magic in the moonlight
It makes you feel quite high
The moonbeams shining down on you
From way up in the sky
There's nothing more romantic
Than to stroll the silvery way
Holding hands with the one you love
And to gaze at the Milky Way.

Pat Robinson
North Lincolnshire

NIGELLA (LOVE -IN-A-MIST)

'Twas last October you passed me by
And even now I wonder why
No look, no smile you gave
Not even a nod or a little wave
Some things have changed
Some things remain the same
But still I am unable . . .
. . . To play this game
Whatever our tomorrow brings
Good, bad or challenging
Wherever happiness lies
I am longing to see you again

The river is deep, the mountain is high
Shouldn't you be by my side?
Wishes and dreams just pie in the sky
Shouldn't we at least have tried?
There are no words - it's unconditional
As deep as the bluest sea
Tears and heartache just melt away
Here in my mind where you are with me
All your foibles buried with time
Have you forgotten all of mine?
It's in the stars to be together
Though higher powers say not forever!

Leisha
Lincolnshire

AUTUMN

Autumn is here,
Russet leaves are falling,
A Maple tree wears a golden crown above a grey-green pillar.
Bare fields after harvest lie barren,
cold with early morning frost.
Monstrous machinery has gone to ground for the winter.
A magpie in a tree,
But only one for sorrow.
I look in vain for another!
Sleepy little animals wait,
Anticipating hibernation.
Twilight comes too soon,
Shortening the daylight hours.
And in December, we'll still remember, gentle autumn days.

Anne Jackson
North Lincolnshire

THE NIGHT

The night wraps around me like a velvet cloak,
Which envelopes me and enables me to soak
In the peace and quiet,
To unwind and drift in the soft velvety constellation,
And to float unhindered aloft in suspended animation.

In the distance, street lights resemble a sparkling necklace,
And the refinery looks like a fairy palace,
Which contrasts to the ugliness of the day,
Speed, pollution, and all shades of grey.

When the night is cold and clear,
The stars pierce through the darkness everywhere,
Outshining the paltry lights made by the human race,
Putting them firmly in their insignificant place.

To some, the night brings an unseen fear
Unless friends and family are near,
I rarely feel afraid in that way
Because I often have that dread during the day.

Marie Walker
Lincolnshire

MERLIN'S POEM

From the Old Ones I came
Down to this tattered earth,
A messenger of Magick.
I have no given name,
Although from demon birth,
I have been known as Merlin.

> From earth's hard core I rose,
> Onto this barren plane,
> A harbinger of Magick.
> I am the one who knows
> All things; I have no name,
> But I am known as Merlin.

From unseen spheres I came
Onto life's tapestry,
An emissary of Magick:
A wizard with no name -
But should you seek for me,
Then I am known as Merlin.

A Brookes
Lincolnshire

THE RIVER TYNE

Dirty, deep, wide flowing river,
as you wend down to the North Sea,
under bridges, by the factories,
decaying houses soon to be
demolished, making way for the new,
like time, you're marching quickly on.
Coursing onward, streaming forward
through the great city built upon
your banks, with ships in days gone by,
passed the castle, the dockyards, mills,
glide undying through my homeland,
from your birth in Cheviot Hills:
To Newcastle down to Tynemouth,
where cherished childhood days were spent.
You will run this way forever,
my flood, my ebb, they're only lent.

Jill Thompson Barker
Lincolnshire

NEW BEGINNINGS

You grew from a seed, sent from above,
A gift from God, a product of love,
When we found out, we jumped for joy,
Will it be a girl or will it be a boy?
From the size of a pea, you continue to grow,
Every tiny finger, every little toe.
The ultrasound pictures showed you were well,
But you've given your poor mum hell,
For the first four months, she was terribly sick,
Now, when she tries to sleep, you move around and kick.
Your life has begun, you've let us know,
There now won't be much longer to go,
Until the expected date of your birth,
When you make your entrance on this earth.
We pray health and happiness will be on your side,
You may find that life is no easy ride,
But we'll all be here, to help you through,
To love, to support, and to guide you.
When you are born, your parents will boast,
To you, dear baby, we'll make a toast,
So let's raise our glasses to new beginnings,
And hopefully, that includes some Lottery winnings!

Andrea Serena Castanha
London

Ode To My Child

You are not yet born, but hear me,
I pray for you against drugs and crime,
You are not yet born, but hear me,
I hope you feel secure during your lifetime.

You are not yet born, but hear me,
I pray for you against false friends,
You are not yet born, but hear me,
I hope that you have good friends.

You are not yet born, but hear me,
I pray that you make the most of your opportunities,
You are not yet born, but hear me,
I wish you all the happiness the world has to bring.

You are not yet born, but hear me,
I pray against debt and money troubles,
You are not yet born, but hear me,
I hope you have a good education.

You are not yet born, but hear me,
I pray that you are healthy,
You are not yet born, but hear me,
I hope that you are wealthy.

You are not yet born, but hear me,
I hope you can cope with the troubles the world throws at you,
You are not yet born, but hear me,
I hope you find a decent job that is suitable for you.

As your mother I write this,
Just to show I care,
With my love I seal this,
Envelope with care.

Claire Murray (15)
Middlesex

A CHANCE OF LOVE

Let me bury my face in your hair
And nuzzle your ear in sweet tenderness that's rare.
Let your lips tremble in pensive anticipation
And not tighten in a grimace of mild irritation.

May your cheeks tinge in pinkish hue
In response to imagined romps that may come true.
But first let us tarry in sweet discourse,
Weaving our way gently to a loving embrace with gathering force.

A loving response will be sought by a tentative kiss or two
As I search for a sign that will be my cue.
Possibly signalled by one of your teasing glances
I shall dare even bolder personal advances.

My hushed and expectant tones will extol my love for you
And an earnest declaration that I will remain eternally true.
May these revelations inspire reciprocal emotions,
Enabling you to provide your deep and lasting devotion.

A Jessop
London

FEBRUARY

Out in the silent garden
with dead leaves all around
the apple tree stands motionless,
as though it waits the sound
of something half forgotten -
a call that once was clear,
but now a fading memory
in the dead month of the year.

No birds fly in the garden,
no leaves adorn the trees,
but as we stand here listening
comes the whisper of a breeze;
and from the earth there rises
that scent new-born each year,
which tells us all so clearly
that spring is almost here.

Ivy Russell
London

FIREWORKS

Scintillating scarlet stars on high,
Golden globes a'gleam from flying light,
Silver showers can stream across the sky.
Orange orbs erupt into a gleaming white.
Soaring streaks assault the blackened frame,
Before descending gently to the floor.
Whirling wheels of light say fixed as lame,
As exploding beacons burst once more.
Noise, confusion, screaming children cry,
Household pets that wish to hide or fly,
Suffer fright, and worse, are often burned.
Careless parents don't obey the rules,
Then the minors suffer 'cause of fools.
Others reap the pain they should've earned.

Z Ryle
London

LIKE A BUTTERFLY

Like a butterfly you flutter on,
Daydreaming,
Fantasising,
Being as creative as you please.

From cocoon to adolescence you slowly emerge,
Stumbling,
Exploring,
Smudging the colours of life.

And when tomorrow comes,
Seeing,
Being,
Facing the challenges that you meet.

And in a tangled web you free yourself,
And stretch out your wings and your aches and pains,
And like a butterfly you flutter on
Through to the very next day.

Sarah Ann Rees
Manchester

FRIENDSHIP

A name which conjures in the eye of man
An all embracing unity of mind
And heart - a chemistry remote, which spans
All men, created such that they might find
In one, the truth that love is God inspired.
It is an angel's dream to hold within
One's hand a chance to share despair in dire
Days; to flow in harmony down mountain
Streams; ride the race of life in amity.
In my uniqueness I have searched amid
The desert wastes of dark calamity,
A shell abandoned with it's heat frigid.
O God that I might find a voice on earth
That sings to me of fondness, warmth and mirth.

Lesley Coates
Merseyside

Country Walk

Lush green meadows pastures new
Buttercups cow parsley too
Acres planted out with maize
Rolling fields where cows could graze
Clematis scrambling through the trees
Hawthorn hedges full of bees
Strolling by the River Wreake
Maxy playing hide and seek
His ears just flapping like two banners
A lovely dog with lovely manners
Climbing over fence and stile
Path of nettles - single file
Suddenly up in a tree
A sparrow hawk with young we see
Fields of hay all freshly mown
Where Max could romp
All on his own
That lovely walk I'll always treasure
Reflect on every step - at leisure.

Barbara Hampson
Merseyside

SHADOWS OF THE WIND

Leaves clatter
Fledglings flutter,
Cobwebs sculpture space.
Pond crinkles mirror chips,
Willow streamers quake.

Windmills turning
Hearthfires burning,
Sycamore seeding space.
Flowers sway and shiver,
Window curtains shake.

Water spuming
Sailboats cleaving.
Seagulls riding space.
Craggy peaks unveiling,
Trees must bend or break.

Nature bows to its passage.
Man reviews its dressage.

Shadows of the wind.

Geoff Gaskill
Norfolk

YESTERDAY

I remember days so long ago, or it could be just in dreams
but happy days were yesterday, or so it always seems

I was running through this woodland path and climbing every tree
and no-one knew about this place, except my friend, my dog and me

This place was always so untouched, or so it would always seem
the tiny path had twists and bends and came out near a stream

A marshland laid behind this steam, with reeds as tall as me
and on the bank there stood alone this giant chestnut tree.

We'd gather nuts and dam the stream and think what fun it's been
and throw a stick for Tess to fetch from within those reeds so green.

I still go back to this special place that only I can see
but now there's only the two of us, just my friend and me

I lost old Tess long long ago and what a pal she'd been
I laid her there beneath that tree beside that tiny stream

I still go back, it's still all there and still the same to me
and I know my friend watches over Tess as he always did with me

But we're still together, just us three, as it's always been
for the memories of yesterday are dearer than any kind of dream

Paul Buckenham
Norfolk

A GIFT

When the daylight slowly falls away
And darkness closes down
All living things upon the earth
Are on journey homeward bound.
Forever when you kneel to pray
For friends that are long gone
Pray that they may live again
Like the sunrise of the morn.

No-one ever waves goodbye
No-one ever dies
they walk along each night and day
They are always at your side.
There they whisper deep
Within your heart and mind
they tell you what to do
And oft times you do wonder
How you managed to pull through.

A contented mind is the greatest gift
A tower of strength and glory.
Like the springtime then
When the flowers come again
To bedeck the whole world over.
Then in life just ponder thus
Reflect on past and present.

Take each day with a cheery smile
It's the golden road to heaven
So remember when
As through life you trend
A golden rule to cherish
A happy heart and peaceful mind
Are gifts of love to treasure.

John Monaghan
Co Tyrone

SILVER WEDDING

After twenty-five years they're still going strong
Two people together, right where they belong,
Two people together as husband and wife
With a love so unique it'll last them for life.

Three children later they've avoided the dangers
Twenty-five years and nothing much changes.
Grandparents now, I'm sure it's been told
Still young at heart they refuse to grow old.

Twenty-five years may seem like forever
But these two people are happy together.
Through good times and bad times, the rough and the smooth
Still going strong they have nothing to lose.

A silver anniversary, the past twenty-five years . . .
Have seen laughter and sadness, the smiles and the tears,
Still standing strong and I'm pretty sure
That they've enjoyed twenty-five years
And they'll enjoy many more.

Margaret Scott
Northumberland

THE LOST VIEW

When I first came to my house, I had a lovely view
Fields dotted with poppies, wild flowers of every hue
There in the distance stood a mighty tree
Beside a path that stretched as far as I could see.

Then a neighbour said to me I've been given to understand
They're going to chop that tree down, build upon the land
Soon a fleet of lorries came and some workers too
It wasn't long before I found I no longer had a view.

But the thing that caused most distress to me
They've built such a great monstrosity
Not neat little houses, with neat little doors
But a concrete block, with fifteen floors.

They've driven away all the lovely wildlife
All I can hear now, is trouble and strife
And now they are building right up to my door
I don't think I like living here anymore.

Mary Shepherd
Nottinghamshire

BARRIERS OF TIME

Across the barriers of time,
My endless love for you
Will keep forever flowing
Till I return to you.
Mere mortal chains can't hold me,
Nor time keep us apart
For you are always with me,
Forever in my heart.
Across the barriers of time,
Death dealt his cruel blow,
Yet even death can't separate
The love we know so well.
Gone from my side, my darling,
But always, oh so near,
Across the barriers of time
Our love will transcend all fear.

Delphine Price
Nottinghamshire

To - Love

Bonaparte was blown apart,
By his love for Josephine.
Prince Edward he became deadwood,
When Wallace could not be queen.
Da Vinci every inch he
Immortalised Mona Lisa.
therefore life without you
Would leave me as dead as
Julius Caesar.

Michael Gardner
Nottinghamshire

THIS LAND

Walk with me through the green fields,
Walk with me through the trees.
Feel the warmth of the sun upon you,
And the coolness on your skin from the breeze.

Let's go to the Island of Lewis
Walk barefoot on the sand.
Then on to our beloved highlands,
Where the heather covers the land.

Come home by the road through Glencoe,
Stop by a crystal stream.
And I'll rest in your tender arms dear,
Whilst we travel this land of dreams.

Take my small hand in your hand,
Love me as never before.
And sheltered in your tender embrace,
Then I'll never ask for more.

M Muirhead
Midlothian

CHANGING WINDS

A gentle breeze blowing,
Tugging mischievously on sails
Of the boats out at sea.
Gradually, it gets more forceful
In it's play with the boats -
Rocking them from side to side
As they bob along on the watery roller-coaster.
Gaining strength with every gust,
The mighty tempest tossing boats
Like playthings in the palm of its hand.
Smashing them against the rocks,
Razor sharp like dragon's teeth,
Until gradually it begins to weaken.
Slackens its grip and retreats,
A gentle breeze once more is blowing.

Gillian Snaith
Tayside

THE HILLS OF SKYE

Let England praise her lakes and fells
and Wales - Mount Snowdon high
and you can kiss the Blarney Stone,
give me the hills of Skye.

Let Paddy praise old Erin's Isle,
give him another try,
when Paddy sings the blarney brings
the smiles to every eye.

Let Welshmen sing their welcome song,
give them another try,
they sing so well, so loud, so high,
they may be heard in Skye.

Let Scotland praise her Rabbie Burns,
his songs and poems, for bye,
let his star shine at every turn
in Shetland and in Skye.

William Hughes
Lothian

I USED TO BE . . .

I used to be married, but now I'm not
I'm asked do I miss it - no, not a lot
Behind closed doors it was really a struggle
Wearing two faces could be quite hard to juggle

I used to be happy, or so I thought
But sadness and an illusion were all that I got
We grew apart, but life still went on
We once were a couple, but then one was gone

I used to be younger, and accept all his patter
But life's what you make it, and age shouldn't matter
It's much more peaceful not worrying about him
My life before - it's beginning to dim

I used to be silent, but now I'm not
I've rediscovered myself and got rid of the rot
I enjoy what I have and ask for no more
I'm getting on with my life, now I've shown him the door

Yes, I used to be married and now I'm not
I'm single, and happy, and that means a lot
Marriage is an institution not to everyone's taste
And all the hurt and anger is such a terrible waste

Edith Clark
Grampian

HOME

Where is your home? They asked us, and to them you replied,
The little cottage down the lane, on the other side.
And so I got to thinking about this place we call our home,
Is it just a place to live, a house of brick and stone?

Or is there a deeper meaning, something more profound,
Than just a small white building on a lonely plot of ground?
Could home be a fireside, a fender, hearth and rug
Sitting together side by side with the one you love?

In my home I can relax and for a little time
I can watch in safety and content the world's troubles can pass by.
And when we have a quarrel, when I am upset,
My home brings to me comfort, it restores my peace and rest.

If life's long journey takes us and many miles we roam,
As long as you are by my side, anywhere is home.
So to me my home is a state of mind, it's not a house or hearth,
It is a well used corner, deep inside your heart.

Heather Parker
Isle of Cumbrae

INNER VISION

I have a heart as big as a mountain
And a mind as deep as the sea
And a soul which would cover the whole of the sky
If I could only love me

I can love most others intensely
And comfort all those in despair
I am the one they can turn to whenever
They know I'll always be there.

But I am my own biggest problem
My self-esteem does not exist
When God was giving out confidence
I feel I have somehow been missed

But I will rise up above this
And tackle each problem I see
For with a bit of faith in myself
I know I can one day love me

I will be a woman of substance
I'll have strength and hope and be fair
I will conquer the weakness inside me
For my warm heart will ever be there.

Valerie Anderson
Midlothian

REFLECTIONS

There's a blue tit in the garden, he's as bonny as can be,
His mate sits in the nesting box hard by the apple tree.
He flits from twig to twig for any insect he can spy,
And chirrs a warning to the world should danger happen by.

He scolds the magpies, cats and crows, and makes it very clear
That I'm as bad as all the rest whenever I appear.
His anger knows no bounds if other blue tits he should see,
And each transgressor's driven from his garden territory.

Bizarrely this wee war-horse has a quirk, he can't ignore
His own reflection in the window and the patio door.
He hurls himself with might and main upon this apparition
Oblivious to the nature of his target of attrition.

You'd think he'd learn quite quickly glass is hard upon the beak,
But this compulsive onslaught has continued for a week!
I've seen, on due reflection, other birds attempt this trick
And they've sussed it out quite quickly. This blue tit's clearly thick!

Alan Ayre
Central

TURNING POINT

They shine so bright, and won't go away
I've tried so hard, both night and day.
one day I'll succumb, laugh and say
'Don't I look *distinguished* now my hair's turned grey?'

Rae Madden
Strathclyde

SOME FACETS OF LOVE

Love, a strange, invisible thing,
Which exhilarates and colours life
In rosy hues, with a tenderness
Reminiscent of a mother's love for her child.
So many small, insignificant happenings
Can trigger love and that flutter in the heart
Which only the receiver notices and to
The world outside, life is no different.

First love, so wonderful, so devastating
When it fails, and ne'er a truer word
Is written, than that a heart can break.
But life goes on, and richer it becomes
With many passing acts of loving kindness.
But when true love emerges, and two
Become a couple, life is more demanding
In consideration for the other half and
More rewarding, even with sacrifice.

With children, life changes and the richness
Grows and overflows so that at times
The loving hurts and almost chokes the
System with its fullness and warmth.
Love in maturing years is so beautiful and expands
With grandchildren and new sons or daughters-in-law,
Demanding tolerance, sensitivity
And hours of patience, kindness and wisdom

Can anyone not be touched by love
When a tiny, warm hand stretches out,
And a tousled head nestles close,
And whispers your name, and 'I love you.'

Elizabeth M Sudder
Kincardineshire

What's That You Said?

Can I run this past you to bring you up to speed?
are we speaking at grass-roots level or talking about a weed?
Are we on a level playing field - does it really matter?
what's happened to our language and good old-fashioned chatter?

Fax, computer, internet, instead of air cargo
voice mail, E-mail, do you remember Wells Fargo?
When you phone to place an order your address they do not need
the postal code is all they want for your goods to arrive with speed.

We've become a nation of numbers and have lost that personal touch
folks converse in rhyming slang - it really is too much
New phrases are born every day - they get me in a lather
I thought to 'take a rain check' meant looking at the weather

No, I can't see where you're coming from - I don't have a crystal ball
this new-fangled language makes no sense to me at all
Why don't we all speak Esperanto with words precise and swift
then we'd all know where we're coming from, if you catch my drift

Helen Urquhart
Perthshire

FRANCES COLLIERY

Frances Colliery once stood proud,
Now there is no sound from underground,
For this pit has been doomed
And for its miners there is gloom.

But these men's memories are long
Even though their jobs are gone.
Thoughts of days gone by
Brings a tear drop to their eyes.

From their memories no-one will erase
Their thoughts of working days.
Under the Firth of Forth they worked
And some of them even got hurt.

With their energy nearly spent,
Returning to the pit shaft they went
With lots of coal still underground,
But now there are no miners to be found.

The pit is closed, the shaft is capped,
But in the future the coal can still be tapped.

Robert Freeman
Fife

HOMELESS

The snow is cold through well worn boots.
When did you have your last warm meal?
You have no place to plant your roots.
Such pain you feel.

Deep down you're sure you hate the rich;
so easy to resent their class,
when all you have is ragged stitch,
You! Good breaks pass.

Tired to your very soul
No place to rest your weary head.
The world for you is very cruel.
Be better dead.

The answer's not in bottle green,
that's not the way for you to live.
I know, for in there I have been;
a real low dive.

Think twice about those you resent,
their lives may not be what it seems.
Perhaps the facade they present
hides broken dreams.

So make the best of what you have.
Put up a fight, rise from the floor.
Your self-esteem you then can save.
Resent no more.

Bill Bardell
Lanarkshire

WHO CREATED CREATION?

Designer and lawyer debated long
Which of them first made a right from a wrong.
The architect made a chaotic earth,
It took a lawyer to give chaos birth,
But the architect's world fell all to bits,
Whilst the lawyer's world was a simple blitz.
So they took their case to the highest court,
And was never a case so fought or fraught.
The architect, in his reticulus,
Had his papers neat and meticulous,
And the judge looked pleased at a case well made
So the lawyer was rather afraid
The decision might go against his side.
he rallied, and with professional pride,
Asked, with impressive *hums* and daunting *ha's*
For further and better particulars.
This threw the architect into a fit,
The judge said 'Here you two, just wait a bit;
Who made the first stuff from which chaos derived?
Now without that stuff you are both deprived
of a leg to stand on, legal, physical -
The whole affair is deeply mystical,
If you don't decide your difference, well,
I'll send the pair of you straight off to H . . . '

Ted Cowen
Shropshire

THE LADY SHOPPER

Her eyes started to wander
For quite a long spell
As she pushed her trolley
Like a bat out of hell
She was looking for bargains
That she could buy
Then bang goes that trolley
Straight into my thigh.

'Cos her eyes were so busy
As she walked around that store
Then five minutes later
Bang, goes her trolley once more
Not a sign of apology
No no not a word
She thought I was a foreigner
By the language she heard.

She'd run into my legs
Then over my toes
I even stopped counting
After three or four goes
So if you meet this lady
Whilst shopping today
Keep your eyes on her trolley
And stay out of harm's way.

Dennis Davies
Shropshire

WHO AM I?

Born to a country? Or born to be free?
After all, mother gave birth where she happened to be.
To my God I'm a person free to visit the earth
But man made the boundaries, ignoring my worth.
We are hounded around and forced to move on
Unwanted, rejected, a problem for some.
But we all have a purpose, desires, hopes and fears,
Let's care for each other, not end all in tears!

Alice Turner
Shropshire

EVERYWHERE I LOOK

I see a poem in a square in a place
and in a child's upturned face.
In a far off country view I see a poem.
In the tiniest flower I see colours true,
orange, yellow, pink and blue.
The spectrum is enormous
and I must tell you too -
That I saw a meteor and shared its beauty
when it shot through a star-lit night.
I see a poem in a sunset in a winter deep in snow,
and when I saw a Peacock butterfly flutter up my
window pane, wings hand painted and washed
by some recent rain,
In that moment, I saw a poem.

P I Bradford
North Somerset

RETURN

Castle is near, I remember it well
Remind me again, yes do please tell
happier times, of peace and content
you sat by my side, you were heaven sent
Crusades came upon us, many travelled away
Should never have gone, departed that day
Castle was yours, your champion charged to protect
Honour beyond reproach, never reason to suspect
Did he fall to your charms, or capture your heart?
I shudder in anger, oh how did it start?
My trusted loyal friend, my queen of all knights
how come this day, on return from those fights
to punish you both, justice be mine
God guide my hand, give me a sign
Lancelot to be cast, from my lands evermore
Guinevere banished, to some foreign shore
My heart is destroyed, my soul it burns
King am I not, Arthur returns!!!

M Perrett
Avon

BYGONES

Many years ago when we were growing up
We never got big presents
We didn't expect too much
An apple and orange in
Our stocking at Xmas time,
New underclothes and we thought that was fine.
What a difference now today
Anything they want, they say.
We had to say our prayers
Kneeling by the bed each night
After all our toys had been put out of sight.
is it better now or is it worse
We never had much money in our purse.
No swearing or at least we must not get caught.
I try to live by the things that I was taught.
We weren't brought up in the land of plenty
but then this was the early twenties.

Dorothy Priddle
Somerset

THEN AND NOW

We carried gas-masks and ID cards.
No street lights, blue lamps in buses and trains.
We gave away railings, and dug up our lawns;
Got little sleep with warnings and planes.

We washed our clothes as we sat in the bath.
The shops ran short of provisions and soap.
We shared our rations and shared our beds.
We gave up everything, all except hope.

We said goodbye to all our boys,
As they left for unknown camps and ports.
Through all our tears we tried to smile,
And not to show our in'most thoughts.

We wrote a letter every day,
'Somewhere in England'; that's all we knew.
But worse than that, once overseas,
Weeks passed, and letters back were few.

We worked all day; fire-watched at night.
No overtime pay; no nine-to-five.
Gave homes to soldiers and evacuees.
We were glad to do it to survive.

The good old days? They certainly were!
We made new friends. People really cared.
We learned new skills and to do without.
We hadn't much, but gladly shared.

We've lost our pride and self-respect;
Our streets are dirty, everywhere neglected.
Our clothes are shabby; nobody cares.
The law and police no longer respected.

How I long for good manners and old-fashioned ways!
How I long to return to the Good Old Days!

Grace Kay
Avon

MIND GAMES

They're all playing mind games,
    They love playing mind games,
        I'm fed up of playing mind games.

Mind games are so complex
Like psychological chess
And yet so very childish
Devoid of all finesse.

Grown-ups relate to grown-ups
In such a primitive way
Full of teenage hang-ups
In their adolescent play.

The foibles of humankind
Ever present since evolution began
Encased like rock in the frail mind,
Most familiar to any mortal man.

I act as an observer
Sitting on the fence of life!
Yet I can see no further
Than the man who beats his wife.

Sex and lies and plain deceit
All thrown in the same mix.
But after passion's burnt with body heat,
The truth hits like a ton of bricks.

They're all playing mind games,
    They love playing mind games,
        Why keep playing mind games?

Richard Hughes
Staffordshire

PEROXIDE AND SILICONE

She apologises for her complexity.
Hoping to hide her intensity.
Covering up her intelligence with peroxide and silicone.
Using a high-pitched voice to hide her uninterested tone.

She manipulates men who lust for her.
Gaining what she wants without falter.
Working her way to the top.
She knows what she wants and she's never gonna stop.

In times of silence she craves conversation.
Disinterest instead of infatuation.
Melodramatically she starts to cry.
Not knowing how much longer she can keep up the lie.

Katrina Austin
Staffordshire

MOTHER

Our mother was a lady,
So good and kind was she
No title ever given her
But duty did exceed.

When we were young,
To her could run
In sickness or in trouble
A smile a word of wisdom heard,
Then all was right in our small world.

So much she gave.
In many ways
No-one could ever take her place.

Time has slipped so swiftly by.
No longer here for when we cry
The songs she sang in years now gone
Are just a memory.

For us still sad.
Try to feel glad
Because I'm sure that she
Is happy in a better place
For all eternity.

Margaret H Mustoe
Suffolk

CRIME AND PUNISHMENT (CHILDHOOD MEMORY)

Memory of a village gang, tomboy yes that was me
Scrumping in Farmer Jones' orchard as dared
Proving to myself, showing lads I was not scared
Like them I would climb the tallest apple tree

'Farmer's coming' gang leader Tom's wailing call
Escaping, pushing past me and letting me fall
No escape for the rest of our gang on that awful day
Only big bully Tom successfully got away

Red faced farmer angered and shouting so fearfully
My ankle was hurting I was frightened and tearful
'Tell him you're hurt' whispered gentle Billy
'Can't do that, the gang will think I'm a silly ninny.'

Lined up before village headmaster brandishing a cane
Shaking as we waited for the strike, the horror, the pain
'So young lady tell my why you are here?
Surely not a gang member, or was this just a dare?'

Our crime was stealing apples, trespassing on private land
Punishment two strikes with the cane on each open hand
That painful incident of long ago haunts me still
Also reminds me of the village and my friend Bill

That day's wrong doing had another memory for me
Recalling the incident of Farmer Jones' apple tree
Getting home with many apples inside my navy knickers
Billy had a good laugh as we exchanged knowing sniggers

K G Johnson
Suffolk

'THE MEANING OF LOVE'

If your heart is ever broken and the world has lost its charms
I'll step in front of you my love, I'll give to you my arms.

If your task is hard and gets too much, the world too cruel to
understand,
I'll be there for as long as you need me, I'll give to you my hands.

If you're weak and sick and lonely and can't see the way to rise,
I'll hold you up and comfort you, I'll give to you my eyes.

If you close your mind in terror and live your life in fear,
I'll stand beside you patiently, I'll give to you my ear.

If you ever feel abandoned with no future but a deep black hole,
Then do not move to hurt yourself, I'll give to you my soul.

If life gets so despondent that you feel you're going to fall,
My love will dry up every tear as I give to you my all.

C Cornwallis
Surrey

SURREY IN APRIL

Under the brow of Juniper Hill
Stands the old grey church by the silent pond
Red-roofed houses and blossoms fill
The stretches of fields to the Downs beyond.
Under the bridges of picturesque time
The Mole glides softly on its way.
Fishermen with rod and line
Wait on the banks to spend the day.
Driving through Surrey at this time of year
The hawthorn's a fuzz and the chestnut's aflame,
Daffodils gone, but the bluebells now here,
Thick in the trees at the side of the lane.
Sunday best for a working city,
Bright and neat and very pretty.

Jo Appleyard
Surrey

SONG OF THE RIVER

I sit and watch the river sliding past
the water flows silently, at ease,
wrapped in its own deep life, intent
to pour into the waiting sea at last.

So many miles from its quiet secret birth
a little bubbling spring, a trickle of water,
a small clear stream murmuring through green fields,
starred with white daisies, close to the earth.

Deepening and broadening it goes on its way
embracing dabbling ducks, stately white swans,
under small bridges, past large busy towns
little boats, big ships, pass in a day.

Small animals make snug homes in its banks
the salmon have come back to clean water
colourful gardens reach down to the water's edge,
folk laze in the sun, lying on its flanks.

Where I sit now the river is strong and wide
dark and deep flowing swiftly through the town.
It flows without cease, without pause,
it will not hesitate nor bide.

The river hurries on, the water that has gone
will never flow by here again,
like the years of life that come and are lost
the river and life journey on.

Marge Chamberlain
Surrey

PASSING TIME

Stealthy years have overtaken
busy restless days.
Follies of youth now vanished,
Sins of middle age a memory.
But yet perfection's goal eludes,
Old age still not ideal.
Other frets and laden sorrows
Hang a heavy yoke.
Frustrations of a failing body,
Jobs once down with ease
Turn quivering flesh
into a pallid mass.
Efforts of the brain grow weak
And memory plays false tricks.
Hearing, sight and touch
Have lost their power.
Vibrant life has flown.
What then to growing old?
Look not back
But leave this sombre world
And rest beneath the sod.

E Dimmock
Surrey

The Timeless Mirror

Looking through the years when I was young,
Into the timeless mirror that is hung,
I see a child who's learning to be wise,
Unblemished skin, alert and sparkling eyes.

I look again, a schoolboy, spotted face.
One who's learning, in the knowledge race.
Homework must be done, no time to play.
The vision in the mirror fades away.

I look again and see a teenage face.
The spots have gone, no more I feel disgrace.
Relaxing in my room and music too.
The mirror fades, the youth has gone from view.

I look again, a young man stares at me.
His smiling face still happy as can be.
Shaving off the whiskers as he goes.
The mirror sees it all, yet no one knows.

I look again and see the years have flown.
The mysteries of life are what you've shown.
Please show me more before my time draws nigh.
You tell the truth and never can you lie.

I look again and see a wrinkled skin.
With time against, I know I cannot win.
Oh mirror tell the secret you have got.
Please tell me why I'm old and you are not.

Stanley Wears
Tyne & Wear

A MORNING WALK

I wander down a once quiet road
Traffic now roaring by
I pass the houses - quiet and still
under the early morning sky

The trees and hedges sparkling with dew
The flowers not yet awake
But always the traffic roaring by
Who has this journey to take?

The rest of the town is still sleeping
The birds just starting to sing
The journeys continue, in lorry and car
taking their driver's near and far
I turn and retrace my steps with a sigh
A once peaceful morning walk is no more
Now that the traffic can go roaring by

M Laverty
Tyne & Wear

TIME FOR CHANGE

What wonders will Earth's man invent,
his problems to resolve
when in his heart there's discontent
and greed, that won't dissolve.

The Change is well upon its way
and getting very near,
which alters years, and time and day
but not man's ways I fear.

The lessons being taught these days,
and ignored by his deaf ears,
sadly reflect man's cruel ways
he's had these thousand years.

What's needed more than a change of date,
is a change in his heart and mind
that demonstrates he's replaced that hate
with a love for all mankind.

Hope, we believe, is eternal,
and to have faith in Him is a must
for our ways we need turn them fraternal,
if the millennium to us He'll entrust.

John Moore
Tyne & Wear

SAVED BY WISE OWL

The winter was cold
The trees were bare, 'twas the middle of the night
An owl sat high on a branch, looking at the sight.

Then suddenly she saw a human on the ground,
screaming for help.
The wise owl thought what she would do
And then decided to sing Tu Whit Tu Woo.

Increasingly she sang
Until the villagers one by one
Awakened by the strong piercing sound
Came to see what all the noise was about.

They saw the poor man lying still in the wood
And carried him to shelter in a nearby abode.

The owl looked on, very pleased with herself
A good deed done for those nice people,
Who only the other day helped her,
When she was caught on a wire.

Time for wise owl to descend from her perch
And hide away from oncoming light,
The beautiful, arrogant, Queen of the night.

Margaret Owen Jones
Wales

'BIG MIG . . . '

The man in the yellow jersey, pushing down hard against the pedal . . .
Fighting, fighting, to keep the pace,
As leader of this, the most famous race . . .

Mountainous hills, winding, twisting roads,
Stretching, it would seem for miles . . .

Feel the pressure, smell the fear,
as the rider fights for his career . . .

The heat is on, the crowds applaud.
Out of his seat the rider rises, for in
his sights the finish line he has set . . .

Heads tucked down, handlebars gripped tight . . .
At last the chance to win this fight . . .

The adrenaline flowing, against the clock, the
rider, somehow, he keeps on going . . .
Past the king of the mountains, the
green points jersey, the youngest
rider, wearing white . . .

To win the 'Tour de France' with ease . . .

S Swift
Clwyd

I'LL KEEP THE LIGHTHOUSE ON

The glue was too weak
To hold our pieces together.
So waltz away anyway,
I'll keep the lighthouse on.

I'll grit my teeth and icily stare,
At my empty canvas with no space spare
For anything but inverted reflections.
I'll keep the lighthouse on.

Smile and nod. Keep yourself mysterious.
Familiarity invites boredom to your doorstep.
Take no clock for granted.
I'll keep the lighthouse on.

And still I rise,
A caged phoenix singing in the ashes.
My poetic license just expired though,
I'll keep the lighthouse on.

Luck is pushed to upper limits
You've found God but won't lend the map
And so I'll venture homeward.
At least the lighthouse is still on.

G Hughes
Mid Glamorgan

THE CALENDAR

Hail, January, we ring in a brand New Year,
The old one has died amidst many a tear;
Then, follows the short month, and soon it is past
Though March can surprise us with its icy blast.

In April the new lambs are starting to strengthen
And daylight is really beginning to lengthen,
The cuckoo'll be here to claim some bird's nest
And many agree that it's really a pest.

Quite soon we've arrived at the fair month of May,
The farmers are ready to harvest the hay;
As June heralds summer, the hols' won't be long
With beaches all set to welcome the throng.

The summery months are now here at last,
The winds and the rains being things of the past,
September is looming, the school bells will ring
But some swallows and swift are still on the wing.

October, November - the nights draw in quickly,
The wintry sun now begins to look sickly,
December - it's Christmas, the time of good cheer
And round comes the cycle to greet the New Year.

T Williams
Carms

PORTHMADOG

This is the place my kinsmen once called home.
This shore shining in the morning light
is filled with ghosts for me.

This is the quay that heard their gruff farewells.
This sea, calling with insistent voice
seduced them with its wiles.

Taciturn men, ithout a backward glance
they went, leaving the ancient mountains
to wait their long return.

Heavy with slate, heading for distant ports,
their ships proudly braved capricious deeps
caressed by wind-flung foam.

Soft panting sails leaned back upon the breeze.
Strong men stirred by stinging-cold salt air
sang through the oceans' space.

Smooth days and rough, they weathered them alike,
constant their love in calmness and storm;
their craft their trusted ark.

Now I visit, a tourist, a stranger,
yet belonging, for my roots are here
in this small seaside town

Its heyday past, its thriving slate trade done.
My fathers too would be strangers here
amid a tourist throng.

The cliffs yet stand, the tide still keeps her tryst;
the siren-sound from the rock still sounds.
Where are the men that hear?

Tall-masted ships sway near the harbour wall;
in summer heat the amorous waves
drowsily woo the land.

Gwenda Owen
East Glamorgan

My Mother's Arms

I'm tucked up tight inside my bed
With fevered brow on fiery head
And under rolling blankets warm
I keep a small and sorry form.

A hushy voice pressed to my ear,
The mother smell is very near,
To ample arms I give myself,
And doze in rocking, silent rest.

My world is quiet, time is mine
And through its precious seconds find
The comfort, in a world of charms,
I'm lost, inside my mother's arms.

S Hollyman
Mid Glamorgan

TOMORROW

Is it time to walk
on scattered shores
feel vibrant air and love
feel strength from cold
and lonely waves
feel hope from dusk above

Is it time to walk
with butterflies
And smile beneath the sun
feel the rays
of peace
And let two hearts
turn into one

Is it time to walk together
under blue clouds
And through grey
Is it time to smile
And close our eyes
To gently light the way

Is it time to find
a strong tree
To carve the love we hide
or time to draw
on golden sand
Await the rushing tide

Rebecca Punter
Mid Glamorgan

YOU

You don't know how much I love you
Or how much I really care
You just look into oblivion
And don't realise I'm there
It's hard for me to look at you
And see your vacant eyes
And know within your far off gaze
Another woman lies
What can I do?
What can I say?
To penetrate your mind
To guide your love towards my own
And to my own love bind

Annie White
South Glamorgan

POOR OMAGH
(A token of remembrance for the victims of the Omagh bombing)

Did you see the tears,
and hear their cries?
did you feel their sorrow
and hear their sighs?
Could you ever begin to understand
how these people felt,
in sad Ireland?,

lives barely begun
were snatched away,
such anguish, and pain,
on that Saturday,
it started with joy,
and ended in terror,
'twill live in our hearts, for ever and ever.

Poor little town,
So full of grief,
where men bow their heads,
and women will weep,
>   Don't let their lives, have been taken in vain,
>   don't let this happen ever again,
>   Tiny white coffins,
>   are not meant to be,
>   *Please let* there be *peace* eternally.

Jacqueline Claire Davies
West Midlands

THE ABORTION

A baby is crying
Alone.
Lying in the field
I see the child
Surrounded by tall blades of grass
But the patch the child is on is bare.

To move close to the child
Is what I want,
To pick up and comfort
To nestle close to my breast
To rightfully drink what the child has been denied.

To reach the baby
I know will never happen,
No matter how hard I try.
For I am being punished
For the crime I have committed.

Crying.
Crying.
The baby continues to cry.
The crying will never stop
As it is my baby,
But at the same time
It is not.

Every night I go to sleep,
I try a little harder to reach the child
To move closer.
But the harder I try,
It moves from me
Further and further away.
And the louder the cries grow.

N B Dahl
West Midlands

THE AQUARIAN

I walk with the wind
And step with the stars
I've played on the moon
And seen Venus from Mars
I've danced with daisies
Uranus is lace
The planet of my birth
All Aquarian's have taste

A planet of creativity
The mind boggles with thought
Far advanced is the Aquarian
Or so I am taught
We live in a world
With free spirit aglow
And the amethyst stone
Is our purple rainbow
The black plains of the
Universe twinkle with diamond
Lights a map of wonder intrigue
And insight
Space, and the universe are
A milkyway to dimensions untold
A galaxy of many
For I am sure we are not alone
It's sheer ignorance to think
That only man are supreme
Beings from another planet
People have seen

Stephanie Brown
West Midlands

ENRAGED BY THE BELL

Ring me, call me, telephone line
'Cause I haven't got a penny and I haven't got a dime
But I gotta get through to my lover on time,
So ring me, call me, telephone line.

Got through to the answerphone, everything fine,
Voice on the other end - simpering whine,
'Hi there, Paul here, gone out to dine.'
So ring me, call me, telephone line.

Stutter when the tone goes, panic on the line,
Can't get the words out, run out of time.
Haven't got the message through, God what a swine!
So ring me, call me, telephone line.

Gone to run a hot bath, wash away the grime,
Soak in foamy bubble bath, tangerine and lime.
Brrr goes the telephone - say it isn't mine!
So ring me, call me, telephone line.

Skid swiftly down the stairs - 'cause they're made of pine,
Trip over me bath towel - legs entwine.
Torn my back badly, x-ray booked for nine!
So they told me by 'phone, on my telephone line.

Telephone's ringing, someone on the line,
Got a heavy breather - valium time!
Said he's got no knickers on - so could he borrow mine?
So I told him what to do with the telephone line.

Heading for a breakdown, counselling time,
Hid under the bedclothes - plenty of wine.
The phone's now disconnected, gone into decline.
Don't ring me *or* call - *no telephone line!*

Shirley Thompson
West Midlands

MOTHER'S LOVE

Look in the mirror
See eyes that shine,
Read yesterday's news
Upon this old face of mine.
You were just a child then
The world at your command,
Yesterday's gone
Time has played its hand.
Did I do all a mother could
I wonder?
I look at you to know.
For in you
I see my own reflection
And I admire you so.
Don't be a stranger
Don't be afraid to ask
Or tell,
Whatever worries you
Worries me as well.
Come back to me
My sweetheart
When you need a hug,
Because there's nothing
In this world like
Undying
Mother's love.

R Ditchfield
West Midlands

YOUNG BOY

Lonely young boy walks down the street,
Thinking quietly, who will he meet?
Gun in his pocket, knife in his hand,
Ready to make his almighty stand.

I have the way, I have the will,
Oh so arrogant, mind on the kill.
One day he'll lose his nerve and the fear,
His life that pattern, oh so clear.

When he's cold his body battered,
Will his young life have really mattered.
To his dear loved ones of course it will.
Don't forget, he's their little boy still.

J Allen
West Midlands

Trees' Seasons

Sudden tremors trees awoke,
as with sap uprisen
confining buds broke
from a shuttered prison.

With primal leaves arrayed
wound their trunks between,
as sun-sparks sprayed
their terraces of green.

In autumn colours stoled
festive banners waved.
Transmuting earth to gold
burnished carpet laid.

Unburdened the trees,
winter strip blown.
Intricate anatomy
of structure shown.

Idris Woodfield
West Sussex

WOMAN

I am not witty, pretty or smart
I am woman with breakable heart
I stand alone within the crowd
No-one sees beneath my shroud
The soul of me cries and dies
No-one sees and no-one tries
I am
Invisible
Cold
Unreal
I am a force as strong as steel
I am
Passion
Warmth
Love
I am woman I rise above

Allison Bishop
West Sussex

CHILDHOOD MEMORIES

As a child laid in bed
Listening to the drones of planes overhead
Patterns of light on the ceiling
Falling to sleep head reeling.

Now as a pensioner laid in bed
The planes again are droning overhead
Refugees plight on my mind
Their suffering pain and new home to find
All those refugees so forlorn
Stop these wars, please no more, no more.

Jan Nolan-Averies
Wiltshire

FOR GRAMPS

Times have been hard,
Times have been sad.
But you were there to support us,
And that's what made us glad.
Your face was never doubtful,
Your love brightly shone.
People went and people came,
And still your love went on.
You gave your most, your all,
You did your very best.
Your courage was most helpful,
Now it's time for you to rest.
But now we are alone,
You have gone to a new life.
But your positive thoughts,
Will always take our strife.
You will be missed more,
Than words can ever say.
But I know you'll watch over us,
Each and every day.
We'll try to be strong,
We won't be too weak.
But at times it will be hard,
And sometimes very bleak.
But I hope it's only Au Revoir,
For a short time,
Because Gramps you're still dear to me,
I'm glad that you were mine.

Kate Boud
Wiltshire

ACCEPTANCE

Where did all those summers go?
As the years go by you think, oh no;
Ageing in body, youthful spirit intact,
So longing to continue, unable to react.
Body and mind confused, but to no avail
Controlled frustration and anger now prevail.
Where once you ran, now you go slow
Reality is such a devastating body blow
Daily is the battle, the torments begin
Youthful spirit and age, the contest to win,
You have to realise they say, you are getting old.
Horrible thought; but the truth must be told.
It's all come too fast, or so it would seem
So slowly unfolding, unawares as a dream.
Silently age engulfs us all, we have to admit
Life's ruthlessly rolling tide and reluctantly submit.
But stop and think of all life's wondrous gifts
Of sight, hearing and speech, so the heart gently lifts.
We might move more slowly, joints not so supple
But we still get around without too much trouble.
Life is a wonderful bonus, gratefully accepted
Thankful for our capabilities, even though belated.

B Pim
Worcestershire

GOATHLAND

Tall wisps of smoke float silently upwards
In the calm still air.
No one stirs, not a soul to be seen,
Neither a whisper to be heard - yet there's life.

Branches bursting into bud
Their tiny shoots a fresh pale green.
Cherry blossoms fill the air, astound the eye,
Their petals shades of pink and white.

High in a tree a blackbird sings
His springtime melody.
His chorus late into the evening rings
With cheerful bursts of song.

Sheep rest gracefully on soft green lawns,
Chewing and basking under warm sunny rays.
Quite unaware of car or rambler.
Amid this quiet sleepy village in the moors.

Geraldine Manfredonia
West Yorkshire

DESTINY

I have new beginning
I have to stop my sinning
I have to use will power
Before it all turns sour

I should use my common sense
Leave the dark and evil fence
Try turn away from this crap
Choose the right road on the map

Turn corners, have a new start
Use my head and not my heart
I always know what is right
And my conscience tries to fight

It never seems to quite work
My conscience will only lurk
It seems I'm not strong enough
To say no and take the rough

It all goes a but Pete' Tong
The right I know just goes wrong
I watch myself I can see
All that's left is destiny

What should have been a fresh start
Ends up as the latest part
Of a life that was once mine
But I chose to decline.

Rebecca Callicot
West Yorkshire

VARIOUS ASPECTS OF YORKSHIRE

Various aspects of Yorkshire
Beauty of the Aysgarth Falls
The scenery of North Yorkshire moors
All God's creation in its splendour.

South Yorkshire
Industries struggle to survive
Some of which now gone
An area of extreme poverty.

Yorkshire people know how to be frugal
Northern communities live with determination
Making do with what we already have
Here in South Yorkshire.

Yorkshire coastline, Robin Hood's Bay
A perfect location for artists
Walks along the Filey Brigg
Long stretches of beach.

Various aspects of Yorkshire
All wonderful in their own way
Some man made
So many wonderful places.

Ian Hammerton
South Yorkshire

THE PERPETUAL ROLLERCOASTER OF LIFE

When we were kids, there were lots of parties,
Trying to see who could eat the most Smarties.
Easter, Birthdays and Christmas were such fun,
Non-stop celebrations, everything merged into one.

Teenagers growing up, discovering all about girls,
Only wearing gear that looked 'cool' to the world.
The ups and downs of courtship and rejection,
Rebelling against your parents ideas of perfection.

Next, the weddings and christenings of family and friends,
Constant buying and wrapping of presents, it never ends.
Your own children grow up and it all starts again,
More faces, more parties, weddings in the rain.

These are the high points that everyone's life brings,
Happy smiling faces that make people's hearts sing.
Then there are the lows, those dark gloomy clouds,
Illness and death of our loved ones, much crying aloud.

As you get older, you realise the stark truth,
More funerals than weddings, means you've lost your youth.
Sombre low-key discussions as you put on the black,
A thinning crowd of faces as the curtains draw back.

D I Muncaster
South Yorkshire

BULLIES, THE SCUM OF THE EARTH

Awake? Why awake when my prayer is to stay asleep,
Slumber brings its comfort, don't waken me to weep,
Where has all my laughter gone, my spirits on a high,
Now that I am all alone, I nightly pray to die.

Each day is the same for me, full of ridicule and scorn,
Making my one wish, that I had never been born,
What have I done to be scorned and abused,
Keeping the bullies and lookers on amused.

Where are my friends I was always pleased to see?
They have joined up with the bullies, who make life hell for me,
As I lie in my bed at the end of the day,
Don't let me wake up is the prayer that I pray.

J Sowersby
North Yorkshire

You Said, You Say

You said you wanted me
Asked if I felt the same
As though it were possible for me
To feel any other way.
Everything about you
A seduction.
You said you wanted me
And my world became bright.

You say you still want me
But now know your mistake
And wish that you had never given voice
To your needs.
This time, you don't ask
How I feel.
You say you still want me
But the comfort there is slight.

Jody Irvine
South Yorkshire

CAT

Probably Burmese,
in silken mottled coat.
He jumps,
light as thistledown,
onto
the aviary.
Fluid of movement
but frustrated,
anticipating breakfast.
Menu
offers choice:-
colour,
flavour,
texture,
old bird or spring chick?
Blue headed lorikeet?
Cockatiel?
Budgerigar
or melodious canary?
Wire separates . . .
Chance
would be a fine thing.

Betty Robertson
North Yorkshire

OUR WORLD

Oh world you are but a symbol of our greed
We all exhaust your wealth, in order to succeed.
The bountiest gifts you offer are far beyond compare
And you are but a grain of sand, in the universe out there.
Hand in hand with the sun and moon, our days and nights are born
As you turn on your axis, whilst we sleep, your journey will greet
the dawn
The wonders that you have performed, mankind cannot perceive
Your elements beneath the ground, have made us rich indeed.
The birth of mankind on your planet, shows what we are in a way
With the knowledge gained through the ages, providing existence today.
But the powers you hold are far greater, than can ever be put into rhyme
For you hold the key, and the purpose, which creates all the tides and
the time.
This world of ours is so precise, can we appreciate what it is worth
Or through blindness destroy ourselves, as well as this beautiful earth
Can man put an end to destruction, by using his skills and his powers
Just by having a greater conception, we'd be saving this planet of ours
Out there in the universe, all planets take their place
Each with its own dimension, all in the vastness of space
Do they encounter the problems, like man has created for you
If there's to be an end of the world, will the universe suffer too.
Imagine our world as a bank, full of wealth and riches untold
We are taking more out, than we put in, should we really be so bold
One day this bank collapses, it has nothing left to give
Only the shell of the building, that's all that's left to live.

Anne Seymour
South Yorkshire

YOU MIGHT . . .

You might be the only one for me,
You might become part of my family tree,
You might have my children, girls and boys,
You might become my plaything, one of my toys,
You might fade out of my life, for all time,
You might break my heart, a heinous crime,
You might kiss and tell, divulge my flaws,
You might halt my life, shut all the doors,
You might become the bane of my life,
You might be nothing but trouble and strife,
You might run away with my best friend,
You might try to send me around the bend,
You might not care about how I feel,
You might hold the cards for you to deal,
You might be the one who ends it all,
You might stick around to watch me fall,
But most of all, only one thing is true,
I will always love you, 'cos you are you.

G N Parkin
South Yorkshire

WORDS LEFT IN STORE

I didn't say I loved you, but
I did.
I didn't say I cared when I should.
I didn't let you know what was trapped
inside my heart.
The importance of words seemed such a
little part.
You are now gone, and the words I should
have said, still trapped inside my head.
You are lost to me, and with you
went the key.

M Rossi
West Yorkshire

REFLECTIONS

Wasn't it only yesterday she sat upon my knee,
that tiny bundle dressed in white I'd hold affectionately.
Wasn't it only yesterday the pacing round and round,
then tuck her in and creep to bed without making a sound.

Wasn't it only yesterday that a toddler she became,
with laughter ringing through the house at every silly game.
Wasn't it only yesterday the scolding then she'd cry,
and promise oh so faithfully, tomorrow she'd really try!

Wasn't it only yesterday exams and all those books,
embarrassment, she'd turn so red at all the admiring looks!
Wasn't it only yesterday you walked her down the aisle,
and I tried so very hard to hide my tears and smile.
Wasn't it only yesterday we gained ourselves a son,
I didn't realise the years have slipped by, one by one.

No it wasn't only yesterday, I'm looking through the book,
that brings back so many memories, all you have to do is look.
But yes, it was only yesterday my daughter and her man,
gave back to me that little girl, for I became a Gran!

Pamela Brannon
Humberside

SUBMISSIONS INVITED
SOMETHING FOR EVERYONE

ANCHOR BOOKS '99 - Any subject,
light-hearted clean fun, nothing unprintable
please.

WOMENSWORDS '99 - Strictly women,
have your say the female way!

STRONGWORDS '99 - Warning!
Age restriction, must be between 16-24,
opinionated and have strong views.
(Not for the faint-hearted)

All poems no longer than 30 lines.
Always welcome! No fee!
Cash Prizes to be won!

Mark your envelope (eg *Poetry Now*) *'99*
Send to:
Forward Press Ltd
Remus House, Coltsfoot Drive
Woodston
Peterborough, PE2 9JX

**OVER £10,000 POETRY PRIZES
TO BE WON!**
Judging will take place in October 1999